CompTIA CySA+ Certification

The Ultimate Study Guide to Practice Questions With Answers and Master the Cybersecurity Analyst Exam

Table of Contents

Introduction

In the dynamic landscape of cybersecurity, where threats evolve at an unprecedented pace, the role of a Cybersecurity Analyst has become increasingly vital. As organizations strive to fortify their digital defenses, professionals equipped with the CompTIA Cybersecurity Analyst (CySA+) certification emerge as indispensable guardians of information security.

This book serves as a comprehensive resource designed to empower individuals preparing for the CySA+ certification. Navigating the complex realm of cybersecurity demands not only theoretical knowledge but also a keen understanding of real-world scenarios. In the pages that follow, you will find a carefully curated collection of practice questions that mirror the intricacies of the CySA+ exam.

Our approach goes beyond rote memorization. Each question has been meticulously crafted to simulate the challenges encountered in the field, providing you with a practical understanding of cybersecurity concepts. The answers provided are not merely solutions; they are detailed explanations that unravel the logic and reasoning behind each choice, enhancing your comprehension and analytical skills.

Success in the CySA+ exam hinges on more than just individual knowledge; it requires the ability to apply that knowledge in diverse situations. This book is your training ground, where theoretical concepts meet real-world problem-solving. Whether you are a seasoned professional seeking certification validation or a newcomer eager to enter the cybersecurity arena, these practice questions offer a valuable opportunity to hone your skills and build the confidence needed to ace the CySA+ exam.

As you embark on this journey, remember that cybersecurity is not just a field of study; it is a dynamic, ever-evolving discipline that demands continuous learning. The quest for the CySA+ certification is not only about passing an exam but about mastering the skills necessary to safeguard digital assets in an interconnected world. Welcome to a learning experience that goes beyond the answers on the page, preparing you to face the challenges of the cybersecurity landscape with resilience and expertise.

Chapter 1: The Importance of Threat Data and Intelligence

In the ever-evolving realm of cybersecurity, the foundation of effective threat and vulnerability management lies in the comprehensive understanding and utilization of threat data and intelligence. This chapter delves into the critical significance of these elements, unraveling the essential building blocks that fortify an organization's defenses.

Foundations of Intelligence:

At the core of threat and vulnerability management lies the concept of intelligence—a dynamic force that empowers cybersecurity professionals to anticipate, mitigate, and respond to threats with precision. Intelligence, in this context, transcends mere information; it embodies the strategic amalgamation of data, context, and analysis.

Understanding the foundations of intelligence is imperative for a cybersecurity analyst. It involves not only recognizing the significance of raw data but also discerning the nuances that transform data into actionable intelligence. Raw data, when processed through the lens of contextual analysis, becomes a powerful tool for predicting potential threats and vulnerabilities.

The first pillar of intelligence is data collection. This encompasses a diverse range of sources, from network logs and endpoint telemetry to open-source intelligence and industry-specific reports. The process involves not only aggregating voluminous data but also discerning its relevance and reliability. A well-rounded cybersecurity analyst possesses the acumen to sift through the noise, extracting meaningful insights from the vast sea of information.

The second pillar involves the analysis of collected data. This step transforms raw information into actionable intelligence by deciphering patterns, anomalies, and potential indicators of compromise. Analysts must develop the ability to connect seemingly unrelated data points, unveiling the narrative behind the numbers. The art of analysis involves understanding the tactics, techniques, and procedures (TTPs) employed by threat actors, enabling proactive defense strategies.

Context is the third pillar that elevates intelligence to a strategic level. Understanding the geopolitical landscape, industry-specific challenges, and the unique threat landscape faced by an organization provides the context necessary to assess the severity and relevance of potential threats. A threat that might be inconsequential in one context could pose a severe risk in another.

In the multifaceted landscape of cybersecurity, effective threat intelligence relies on a diverse array of sources. This section explores the richness and complexity of these intelligence sources, emphasizing the need for a comprehensive approach to information gathering.

Open-Source Intelligence (OSINT): OSINT serves as a foundational pillar, leveraging publicly available information to glean insights into potential threats. Analysts tap into online forums, social media, and public databases to gather data that contributes to a broader understanding of the threat landscape.

Technical Intelligence (TECHINT): This source focuses on the technical aspects of threat intelligence. It involves the analysis of malware, vulnerabilities, and exploits, providing a deep dive into the tools and techniques employed by threat actors. TECHINT equips analysts with the knowledge needed to fortify defenses against specific cyber threats.

Human Intelligence (HUMINT): The human element remains crucial in the world of cybersecurity. HUMINT involves information obtained through direct interaction with individuals, whether through interviews, conversations, or other interpersonal means. This source adds a nuanced layer to threat intelligence by incorporating human insights and perspectives.

Cybersecurity Vendor Reports: Companies specializing in cybersecurity often release reports based on their research and findings. These reports offer valuable insights into emerging threats, vulnerabilities, and attack trends. Analysts leverage these vendor reports to stay abreast of the latest developments in the threat landscape.

Government and Law Enforcement Agencies: Collaboration with government entities and law enforcement agencies provides access to classified intelligence. Information shared by these entities can offer a broader perspective on national and international threats, enabling organizations to align their defenses with larger security initiatives.

Understanding the diverse nature of intelligence sources is paramount for a well-rounded cybersecurity analyst. The ability to synthesize information from various channels enhances the accuracy and comprehensiveness of threat intelligence, enabling proactive defense measures.

Confidence Levels:

As cybersecurity analysts assess threat intelligence, assigning confidence levels becomes instrumental in decision-making. This section explores the nuances of confidence levels, emphasizing their role in gauging the reliability and credibility of intelligence.

High Confidence: Intelligence with a high confidence level is characterized by strong supporting evidence and a high degree of certainty. Analysts can rely on this information to make informed decisions, implement countermeasures, and allocate resources effectively.

Moderate Confidence: Moderate confidence indicates a reasonable level of supporting evidence but may still have some gaps or uncertainties. Analysts may proceed with caution, implementing measures while remaining vigilant for additional corroborating information.

Low Confidence: Intelligence with a low confidence level lacks substantial supporting evidence or is based on unverified information. Analysts treat this information with skepticism, using it as a starting point for further investigation rather than taking immediate action.

Understanding confidence levels is crucial for prioritizing and responding to threats effectively. A nuanced evaluation ensures that resources are allocated appropriately, and response strategies align with the reliability of the intelligence at hand.

Indicator Management:

Indicators are the breadcrumbs that lead cybersecurity analysts to potential threats. This section delves into the intricacies of indicator management, emphasizing the need for a systematic approach to handle these crucial pieces of information.

Indicators of Compromise (IoCs): IoCs are artifacts or patterns that suggest a system has been compromised. These include suspicious files, network traffic anomalies, or unexpected system behavior. Effectively managing IoCs involves timely detection, analysis, and response to mitigate potential damage.

Indicators of Attack (IoAs): IoAs provide insight into the tactics, techniques, and procedures (TTPs) employed by threat actors. Recognizing IoAs allows analysts to identify potential threats based on the methods adversaries use, enabling proactive defense strategies.

Indicators of Reconnaissance: Threat actors often engage in reconnaissance activities before launching an attack. Managing indicators of reconnaissance involves monitoring and analyzing activities such as scanning, probing, and information gathering, providing early warning signs of potential threats.

Indicators of Vulnerability: These indicators highlight potential weaknesses within a system. Effective management involves identifying and addressing vulnerabilities promptly to prevent exploitation by threat actors.

A robust indicator management process is essential for a proactive cybersecurity stance. This section equips analysts with the knowledge and methodologies needed to systematically handle indicators, enhancing the organization's ability to detect and respond to threats in a timely and effective manner.

Threat Classification:

Threat classification forms the bedrock of understanding and mitigating cybersecurity risks. In this section, we delve into the taxonomy of threats, categorizing them to provide clarity and insight into the diverse challenges faced by cybersecurity professionals.

Malware Threats: Malicious software, or malware, poses a pervasive threat to digital ecosystems. This category includes viruses, worms, Trojans, ransomware, and other types of code designed to compromise systems, steal information, or disrupt operations.

Network-Based Threats: Threats originating from the network encompass various attacks such as Distributed Denial of Service (DDoS), Man-in-the-Middle (MitM), and packet-sniffing attacks. Understanding these threats is crucial for safeguarding the integrity and availability of network resources.

Web-Based Threats: Cyber threats frequently exploit vulnerabilities in web applications and browsers. This category includes cross-site scripting (XSS), SQL injection, and other web-based attacks that can compromise sensitive data or facilitate unauthorized access.

Social Engineering Attacks: Threats targeting human psychology to manipulate individuals into divulging confidential information or performing actions against their own interests fall under social engineering. Phishing, pretexting, and baiting are examples of such attacks.

Insider Threats: Threats originating from within an organization pose unique challenges. These can be intentional or unintentional, involving employees, contractors, or other trusted entities compromising security either knowingly or unknowingly.

Understanding threat classification is pivotal for crafting a robust defense strategy. By categorizing threats, cybersecurity professionals can tailor their approach to address specific vulnerabilities and risks, fortifying their organization against a spectrum of potential attacks.

Threat Actors:

The landscape of cybersecurity is shaped by a diverse array of threat actors, each with distinct motivations, capabilities, and tactics. This section provides an insight into the various personas that perpetrate cyber threats.

Nation-State Actors: Governments or state-sponsored entities engage in cyber activities for political, economic, or military purposes. Their advanced capabilities often involve sophisticated attacks targeting other nations, critical infrastructure, or intellectual property.

Hacktivists: Driven by ideological or political motivations, hacktivists aim to promote their agenda through cyber means. Their attacks may target organizations, government entities, or individuals perceived as adversaries.

Cybercriminals: Motivated by financial gain, cybercriminals engage in activities such as data theft, ransomware attacks, and identity theft. Their tactics range from deploying sophisticated malware to conducting online fraud and extortion.

Insiders: Individuals within an organization, whether employees or contractors, can pose a significant threat. Insiders may compromise security intentionally or unintentionally, making them a challenging category to address.

Script Kiddies: Novice hackers, often motivated by curiosity or a desire for recognition, fall into the script kiddie category. While lacking advanced skills, they may still cause disruptions through the use of readily available hacking tools.

Understanding the motivations and characteristics of threat actors is essential for developing effective defense strategies. Tailoring cybersecurity measures to anticipate and counteract the specific tactics employed by different threat personas enhances the overall resilience of an organization.

Intelligence Cycle:

The intelligence cycle represents a systematic process through which organizations collect, analyze, and disseminate intelligence to enhance their cybersecurity posture. This section outlines the key stages of the intelligence cycle.

Planning and Direction: The intelligence cycle begins with defining objectives, priorities, and requirements. This stage involves setting the scope of intelligence activities to align with organizational goals and security needs.

Collection: In this stage, relevant data and information are gathered from various sources, including open-source intelligence, technical sources, and human intelligence. The goal is to assemble a comprehensive dataset for analysis.

Processing: Collected data undergoes processing to convert raw information into a format suitable for analysis. This may involve sorting, organizing, and validating the data to ensure its accuracy and relevance.

Analysis and Production: Analysts dissect the processed information, identifying patterns, correlations, and potential threats. The goal is to distill actionable intelligence that informs decision-making and proactive security measures.

Dissemination: Once analyzed, intelligence is disseminated to relevant stakeholders within the organization. Timely and accurate communication is crucial to prompt decision-making and the implementation of effective security measures.

Feedback: The intelligence cycle incorporates a feedback loop where insights gained from the analysis and response efforts are used to refine and improve future intelligence activities. This iterative process enhances the organization's overall resilience.

Understanding and implementing the intelligence cycle empowers organizations to proactively address emerging threats. By systematically collecting, analyzing, and disseminating intelligence, cybersecurity professionals can stay ahead of potential risks, fostering a dynamic and adaptive security posture.

Commodity Malware:

Commodity malware represents a category of malicious software that is widely available and often used by multiple threat actors. This section explores the characteristics and implications of commodity malware within the cybersecurity landscape.

Commonality: Commodity malware is characterized by its ubiquity and accessibility. It is not bespoke or tailored to a specific target but rather designed for widespread use against a broad range of potential victims.

Distribution Channels: Commodity malware is often distributed through common channels such as malicious websites, phishing emails, or compromised software. Its widespread availability makes it a preferred choice for attackers seeking ease of deployment.

Generic Exploitation: Unlike targeted malware designed for specific vulnerabilities or organizations, commodity malware exploits common vulnerabilities that may exist across a broad spectrum of systems. This makes it a versatile tool for cybercriminals.

Payload Variety: Commodity malware can encompass a range of malicious payloads, including ransomware, keyloggers, and botnets. Its versatility allows threat actors to adapt their tactics based on their objectives.

Low Cost of Entry: The accessibility and low cost associated with commodity malware make it an attractive option for various threat actors, including those with limited resources or sophistication. This democratization of malicious tools contributes to the overall cyber threat landscape.

Understanding commodity malware is essential for organizations aiming to bolster their defenses. By recognizing the patterns and characteristics associated with these widely used threats, cybersecurity professionals can implement proactive measures to mitigate the risks posed by these ubiquitous malicious tools.

Practice Question and Answers

Question: What is the primary purpose of collecting open-source intelligence (OSINT) in cybersecurity?

a) To secure classified government information

b) To gather information from publicly available sources

c) To identify insider threats within an organization

d) To conduct vulnerability assessments

Answer: b) To gather information from publicly available sources

Explanation: Open-source intelligence (OSINT) involves collecting information from publicly accessible sources. This includes data from the internet, social media, and public databases, providing a broader understanding of the threat landscape.

Question: What is the significance of confidence levels in threat intelligence?

a) They determine the severity of the threat

b) They indicate the likelihood of an attack

c) They assess the reliability and credibility of intelligence

d) They prioritize threat response actions

Answer: c) They assess the reliability and credibility of intelligence

Explanation: Confidence levels help cybersecurity analysts gauge the reliability and credibility of threat intelligence. High confidence indicates strong supporting evidence, while low confidence suggests a lack of substantial evidence.

Question: Why is it crucial to recognize indicators of compromise (IoCs) promptly?

a) To identify threat actors

b) To prevent data breaches

c) To allocate resources effectively

d) To enhance the intelligence cycle

Answer: b) To prevent data breaches

Explanation: Recognizing indicators of compromise (IoCs) promptly allows organizations to take immediate action to prevent data breaches or other malicious activities, mitigating potential damage.

Question: What characterizes intelligence with a low confidence level?

a) Strong supporting evidence

b) Moderate certainty

c) Lack of substantial supporting evidence

d) High reliability

Answer: c) Lack of substantial supporting evidence

Explanation: Intelligence with a low confidence level lacks substantial supporting evidence, indicating a need for caution and further investigation before taking decisive actions.

Question: How do cybersecurity professionals benefit from the intelligence cycle?

a) By planning and directing attacks

b) By disseminating information only

c) By systematically managing threat intelligence

d) By ignoring feedback loops

Answer: c) By systematically managing threat intelligence

Explanation: The intelligence cycle helps cybersecurity professionals systematically collect, analyze, and disseminate threat intelligence, enhancing their ability to address emerging risks and vulnerabilities.

Question: What distinguishes commodity malware from targeted malware?

a) Commonality and ubiquity

b) Specificity to a target

c) Exploitation of zero-day vulnerabilities

d) Government-sponsored deployment

Answer: a) Commonality and ubiquity

Explanation: Commodity malware is characterized by its commonality and widespread availability, making it distinct from targeted malware designed for specific vulnerabilities or organizations.

Question: In threat classification, what do social engineering attacks primarily target?

a) Network vulnerabilities

b) Human psychology

c) Insider threats

d) Web-based applications

Answer: b) Human psychology

Explanation: Social engineering attacks primarily target human psychology to manipulate individuals into divulging confidential information or performing actions against their own interests.

Question: How do hacktivists differ from cybercriminals?

a) Motivations for financial gain

b) Sophistication of attacks

c) Use of commodity malware

d) Ideological or political motivations

Answer: d) Ideological or political motivations

Explanation: Hacktivists are motivated by ideological or political goals, whereas cybercriminals are primarily driven by the desire for financial gain through activities like data theft and online fraud.

Question: What is the main objective of the processing stage in the intelligence cycle?

a) Collection of raw data

b) Validation of information accuracy

c) Analysis of potential threats

d) Conversion of raw data into a usable format

Answer: d) Conversion of raw data into a usable format

Explanation: The processing stage involves converting raw data into a format suitable for analysis, ensuring that information is organized and validated for accuracy.

Question: Why is insider threat considered a unique challenge in cybersecurity?

a) Lack of technological defenses

b) Inability to identify insider threats

c) Intentional or unintentional compromise by trusted entities

d) Exclusive targeting of government organizations

Answer: c) Intentional or unintentional compromise by trusted entities

Explanation: Insider threats involve individuals within an organization, such as employees or contractors, compromising security intentionally or unintentionally, posing a unique challenge in cybersecurity.

Question: What is the primary focus of technical intelligence (TECHINT) in cybersecurity?

a) Analysis of network traffic

b) Understanding human psychology

c) Examination of malware and exploits

d) Gathering information from publicly available sources

Answer: c) Examination of malware and exploits

Explanation: Technical intelligence (TECHINT) focuses on the technical aspects of threat intelligence, involving the analysis of malware, vulnerabilities, and exploits.

Question: How does the intelligence cycle contribute to an organization's resilience?

a) By planning and directing intelligence activities

b) By providing feedback on threat responses

c) By systematically managing threat intelligence

d) By solely disseminating intelligence to stakeholders

Answer: c) By systematically managing threat intelligence

Explanation: The intelligence cycle contributes to an organization's resilience by systematically managing threat intelligence, allowing for proactive responses to emerging threats.

Question: What role does context play in the intelligence cycle?

a) Organizing raw data

b) Determining severity of threats

c) Providing background information

d) Synthesizing intelligence reports

Answer: b) Determining severity of threats

Explanation: Context in the intelligence cycle plays a crucial role in determining the severity and relevance of potential threats, helping analysts assess the impact on the organization.

Question: What distinguishes indicators of attack (IoAs) from indicators of compromise (IoCs)?

a) Source of information

b) Time of occurrence

c) Types of malicious activities

d) Level of confidence

Answer: c) Types of malicious activities

Explanation: Indicators of attack (IoAs) focus on the tactics, techniques, and procedures (TTPs) employed by threat actors, distinguishing them by the types of malicious activities rather than specific artifacts.

Question: How do government and law enforcement agency reports contribute to threat intelligence?

a) By providing classified intelligence only

b) By offering insights into industry-specific challenges

c) By creating unnecessary complexity in threat analysis

d) By restricting information sharing

Answer: b) By offering insights into industry-specific challenges

Explanation: Government and law enforcement agency reports contribute to threat intelligence by offering insights into industry-specific challenges, helping organizations align their defenses with larger security initiatives.

Question: What is the primary objective of the intelligence cycle's feedback loop?

a) To plan and direct future intelligence activities

b) To validate the accuracy of collected data

c) To enhance the analysis and production stage

d) To refine and improve future intelligence activities

Answer: d) To refine and improve future intelligence activities

Explanation: The feedback loop in the intelligence cycle serves to refine and improve future intelligence activities by incorporating insights gained from analysis and response efforts.

Question: In threat classification, what defines network-based threats?

a) Attacks on web applications

b) Threats originating from within an organization

c) Exploitation of network vulnerabilities

d) Attacks on human psychology

Answer: c) Exploitation of network vulnerabilities

Explanation: Network-based threats involve attacks that exploit vulnerabilities within the network, such as Distributed Denial of Service (DDoS) or Man-in-the-Middle (MitM) attacks.

Question: Why is understanding the geopolitical landscape crucial for threat intelligence?

a) To plan political campaigns

b) To identify insider threats

c) To assess the severity of threats

d) To launch international cyberattacks

Answer: c) To assess the severity of threats

Explanation: Understanding the geopolitical landscape is crucial for assessing the severity and relevance of potential threats in the context of international relations and security dynamics.

Question: What makes script kiddies distinct in the threat actor landscape?

a) Motivated by financial gain

b) Lack of hacking skills

c) Government sponsorship

d) Advanced use of sophisticated tools

Answer: b) Lack of hacking skills

Explanation: Script kiddies are characterized by their lack of advanced hacking skills. They often rely on readily available hacking tools and are motivated by curiosity or a desire for recognition.

Question: How does the intelligence cycle contribute to decision-making in cybersecurity?

a) By disseminating information only

b) By providing feedback on threat responses

c) By systematically managing threat intelligence

d) By planning and directing intelligence activities

Answer: c) By systematically managing threat intelligence

Explanation: The intelligence cycle contributes to decision-making by systematically managing threat intelligence, allowing organizations to make informed decisions based on comprehensive analysis.

Question: What is the primary goal of insider threat detection in cybersecurity?

a) To identify vulnerabilities in the network

b) To prevent insider threats from occurring

c) To analyze patterns of network traffic

d) To assess the geopolitical landscape

Answer: b) To prevent insider threats from occurring

Explanation: The primary goal of insider threat detection is to prevent insider threats from occurring by identifying and addressing potential risks posed by individuals within the organization.

Question: How do cybercriminals differ from nation-state actors in terms of motivation?

a) Cybercriminals focus on financial gain, while nation-state actors are politically motivated

b) Nation-state actors focus on financial gain, while cybercriminals are politically motivated

c) Both cybercriminals and nation-state actors are solely motivated by financial gain

d) Both cybercriminals and nation-state actors are solely politically motivated

Answer: a) Cybercriminals focus on financial gain, while nation-state actors are politically motivated

Explanation: Cybercriminals are primarily motivated by financial gain, while nation-state actors engage in cyber activities for political, economic, or military purposes.

Question: Why is the processing stage essential in the intelligence cycle?

a) To plan and direct intelligence activities

b) To convert raw data into a usable format for analysis

c) To provide feedback on threat responses

d) To validate the accuracy of collected data

Answer: b) To convert raw data into a usable format for analysis

Explanation: The processing stage is essential in the intelligence cycle to convert raw data into a usable format suitable for analysis, ensuring organized and validated information.

Question: What defines hacktivists in the realm of threat actors?

a) Motivated by financial gain

b) Lack of hacking skills

c) Advanced use of sophisticated tools

d) Ideological or political motivations

Answer: d) Ideological or political motivations

Explanation: Hacktivists are characterized by their ideological or political motivations, distinguishing them from threat actors primarily motivated by financial gain.

Question: In threat classification, what characterizes web-based threats?

a) Attacks on network vulnerabilities

b) Exploitation of human psychology

c) Attacks on web applications

d) Insider threats

Answer: c) Attacks on web applications

Explanation: Web-based threats involve attacks that exploit vulnerabilities in web applications and browsers, compromising sensitive data or facilitating unauthorized access.

Question: How do script kiddies impact the cyber threat landscape?

a) They contribute to advanced cyber attacks

b) They lack hacking skills and use readily available tools

c) They are exclusively sponsored by governments

d) They focus on politically motivated activities

Answer: b) They lack hacking skills and use readily available tools

Explanation: Script kiddies impact the cyber threat landscape by lacking advanced hacking skills and relying on readily available tools, often motivated by curiosity or a desire for recognition.

Question: What distinguishes indicators of vulnerability within the context of cybersecurity?

a) They identify weaknesses within a system

b) They focus on patterns of network traffic

c) They indicate ongoing cyber attacks

d) They are specific to a target

Answer: a) They identify weaknesses within a system

Explanation: Indicators of vulnerability identify potential weaknesses within a system, allowing organizations to address and mitigate these vulnerabilities promptly.

Question: Why is the feedback loop an integral part of the intelligence cycle?

a) To plan and direct future intelligence activities

b) To provide context for threat intelligence

c) To convert raw data into a usable format

d) To assess the reliability of intelligence

Answer: a) To plan and direct future intelligence activities

Explanation: The feedback loop in the intelligence cycle is integral to plan and direct future intelligence activities, allowing organizations to refine and improve their approach based on insights gained from analysis and response efforts.

Question: What role does the dissemination stage play in the intelligence cycle?

a) To plan and direct future intelligence activities

b) To refine and improve future intelligence activities

c) To systematically manage threat intelligence

d) To communicate intelligence to relevant stakeholders

Answer: d) To communicate intelligence to relevant stakeholders

Explanation: The dissemination stage in the intelligence cycle involves communicating intelligence to relevant stakeholders within the organization, facilitating timely decision-making and response.

Question: What distinguishes social engineering attacks in the realm of threat classification?

a) Exploitation of network vulnerabilities

b) Attacks on web applications

c) Targeting of human psychology

d) Use of advanced hacking tools

Answer: c) Targeting of human psychology

Explanation: Social engineering attacks distinguish themselves by targeting human psychology to manipulate individuals into divulging confidential information or performing actions against their own interests.

Chapter 2: Threat Intelligence in Support of Organizational Security

Levels of Intelligence:

In the dynamic landscape of cybersecurity, understanding the levels of intelligence is paramount for organizations aiming to fortify their security posture. This chapter delves into the intricacies of intelligence levels, offering insights into how varying degrees of granularity empower cybersecurity professionals in their quest to safeguard organizational assets.

Strategic Intelligence:

Definition: Strategic intelligence provides a high-level view of the threat landscape, focusing on long-term trends, geopolitical factors, and overarching risks. It aids organizational leaders in making informed decisions related to security investments, resource allocation, and overarching security policies.

Application: By comprehending the strategic intelligence landscape, organizations can align their security strategies with broader business objectives and anticipate potential threats that may arise over extended periods.

Operational Intelligence:

Definition: Operational intelligence operates at an intermediate level, providing insights into current threats, ongoing attack campaigns, and specific vulnerabilities. It aids security teams in developing and adjusting day-to-day strategies to address immediate risks.

Application: Operational intelligence enables timely responses to active threats, allowing security teams to prioritize and deploy countermeasures effectively. It serves as a bridge between strategic insights and tactical responses.

Tactical Intelligence:

Definition: Tactical intelligence focuses on specific details related to cyber threats, such as the tactics, techniques, and procedures (TTPs) employed by threat actors. It assists security practitioners in crafting targeted responses to active threats.

Application: By understanding the specific methods employed by threat actors, organizations can enhance their detection and mitigation capabilities. Tactical intelligence is instrumental in shaping day-to-day security operations.

Technical Intelligence (TechINT):

Definition: Technical intelligence delves into the intricate details of cyber threats, including the analysis of malware, vulnerabilities, and technical indicators. It equips security analysts with in-depth knowledge to identify and counter specific technical aspects of threats.

Application: TechINT enhances an organization's ability to defend against sophisticated threats by providing granular technical details. It empowers cybersecurity professionals to implement targeted security measures.

Human Intelligence (HumINT):

Definition: Human intelligence involves insights gained through direct interaction with individuals or entities involved in cyber threats. It provides a human-centric perspective on threat actors, their motivations, and potential insider threats.

Application: HumINT enhances the understanding of threat actors' motivations and intentions. It enables organizations to tailor security strategies to address human-driven vulnerabilities and social engineering threats.

Understanding and leveraging these levels of intelligence empower organizations to build a comprehensive threat intelligence framework. Strategic insights inform overarching security strategies, while tactical and technical details guide day-to-day operations. Operational and human intelligence provide a bridge between the high-level strategic view and the granular details necessary for effective cybersecurity defense.

As organizations navigate the ever-evolving threat landscape, the integration of these intelligence levels becomes instrumental in establishing a resilient and adaptive security posture. This chapter unravels the layers of intelligence, equipping cybersecurity professionals with the knowledge needed to harness the full spectrum of threat intelligence in support of organizational security.

Attack Frameworks:

In the perpetual chess match between cybersecurity professionals and threat actors, understanding attack frameworks is pivotal. This chapter explores the intricacies of attack frameworks, providing a comprehensive view of the tools and tactics employed by adversaries to breach organizational defenses.

MITRE ATT&CK Framework:

Overview: The MITRE ATT&CK framework is a comprehensive matrix that outlines the tactics, techniques, and procedures (TTPs) utilized by threat actors during various stages of the cyber kill chain.

Application: Security professionals leverage the MITRE ATT&CK framework to enhance threat detection, incident response, and threat intelligence sharing. It serves as a universal language for describing cyber threats.

Kill Chain Framework:

Overview: The kill chain framework breaks down the stages of a cyber attack, from initial reconnaissance to data exfiltration. Understanding this sequential process aids in developing proactive defense strategies.

Application: By aligning defenses with each stage of the kill chain, organizations can detect and disrupt attacks at various points, preventing adversaries from progressing to advanced stages.

Diamond Model of Intrusion Analysis:

Overview: The Diamond Model analyzes cyber intrusions by considering the Adversary, Infrastructure, Capability, and Victim perspectives. It provides a structured framework for comprehending the dynamics of cyber threats.

Application: The Diamond Model enhances threat intelligence analysis, allowing security analysts to connect disparate pieces of information and gain a holistic understanding of cyber threats.

Threat Research:

In the ever-evolving landscape of cybersecurity, staying ahead of emerging threats requires a commitment to continuous threat research. This section delves into the methodologies and practices that underpin effective threat research.

Open-Source Intelligence (OSINT) Research:

Methodology: OSINT research involves collecting information from publicly available sources. Analysts utilize online forums, social media, and other accessible platforms to gather insights into potential threats.

Application: OSINT research provides a foundational layer for threat intelligence, offering a broader understanding of the threat landscape and potential indicators of compromise.

Reverse Engineering:

Methodology: Reverse engineering involves dissecting malware or other malicious artifacts to understand their inner workings. This process unveils the functionality, vulnerabilities, and potential countermeasures against specific threats.

Application: Security researchers use reverse engineering to analyze and mitigate the impact of malware, contributing to the development of robust defense mechanisms.

Threat Modeling Methodologies:

Threat modeling is a proactive approach to identify and mitigate potential security vulnerabilities. This chapter explores diverse threat modeling methodologies that guide organizations in systematically assessing and addressing security risks.

STRIDE Model:

Overview: The STRIDE model categorizes threats based on six dimensions - Spoofing, Tampering, Repudiation, Information Disclosure, Denial of Service, and Elevation of Privilege. It provides a structured way to identify potential security threats.

Application: Organizations leverage the STRIDE model to systematically assess the security implications of their systems and applications, guiding the implementation of appropriate security controls.

DREAD Model:

Overview: The DREAD model assesses threats based on five attributes - Damage, Reproducibility, Exploitability, Affected Users, and Discoverability. This approach helps prioritize and focus efforts on addressing the most critical threats.

Application: Security professionals use the DREAD model to evaluate the potential impact and likelihood of threats, aiding in the prioritization of security measures.

Threat Intelligence Sharing with Supported Functions:

Effective threat intelligence is a collaborative effort, and sharing insights with relevant stakeholders strengthens the overall security posture. This section explores the practices of sharing threat intelligence and its integration with supported functions.

Information Sharing and Analysis Centers (ISACs):

Overview: ISACs facilitate the sharing of threat intelligence among organizations within specific industries. They serve as collaborative platforms where members share insights, trends, and mitigation strategies.

Integration: Organizations participating in ISACs benefit from collective intelligence, gaining insights into industry-specific threats and enhancing their ability to preemptively defend against emerging risks.

Collaboration with Law Enforcement:

Overview: Collaborating with law enforcement agencies enhances threat intelligence by providing access to classified information and the legal framework to address cyber-crime. This partnership supports investigations and mitigates threats at a broader level.

Integration: Organizations working in tandem with law enforcement agencies contribute to a safer cyber landscape by actively participating in the identification and apprehension of cybercriminals.

As organizations navigate the intricate realm of advanced cybersecurity practices, understanding attack frameworks, engaging in continuous threat research, adopting robust threat modeling methodologies, and embracing collaborative threat intelligence sharing become pivotal components of a proactive and resilient security strategy. This chapter equips cybersecurity professionals with the knowledge and methodologies needed to stay ahead of evolving threats and bolster organizational defenses.

Practice Questions and Answers

Question: What is the primary purpose of strategic intelligence in the context of organizational security?

a) To provide detailed technical insights

b) To focus on day-to-day threat responses

c) To inform long-term security strategies

d) To analyze specific attack tactics

Answer: c) To inform long-term security strategies

Explanation: Strategic intelligence provides a high-level view, informing long-term security strategies and aligning them with broader business objectives.

Question: How does the MITRE ATT&CK framework contribute to threat intelligence?

a) By providing a high-level view of geopolitical factors

b) By describing cyber threats in a universal language

c) By focusing on day-to-day threat responses

d) By analyzing specific attack tactics

Answer: b) By describing cyber threats in a universal language

Explanation: The MITRE ATT&CK framework serves as a universal language for describing cyber threats, aiding in threat intelligence sharing and analysis.

Question: What distinguishes operational intelligence from strategic intelligence?

a) Operational intelligence focuses on long-term trends

b) Operational intelligence is universal, while strategic is industry-specific

c) Operational intelligence addresses day-to-day threats

d) Operational intelligence primarily analyzes geopolitical factors

Answer: c) Operational intelligence addresses day-to-day threats

Explanation: Operational intelligence focuses on current threats and aids in day-to-day threat responses.

Question: How does the Diamond Model of Intrusion Analysis contribute to understanding cyber threats?

a) By providing insights into long-term trends

b) By breaking down the stages of a cyber attack

c) By analyzing the Adversary, Infrastructure, Capability, and Victim perspectives

d) By focusing on specific attack tactics

Answer: c) By analyzing the Adversary, Infrastructure, Capability, and Victim perspectives

Explanation: The Diamond Model provides a structured framework for understanding cyber threats by analyzing multiple perspectives.

Question: What role does human intelligence (HumINT) play in threat intelligence?

a) Analyzing malware and technical indicators

b) Providing insights into human-centric aspects of threat actors

c) Describing cyber threats in a universal language

d) Assessing day-to-day threat responses

Answer: b) Providing insights into human-centric aspects of threat actors

Explanation: HumINT provides insights into the motivations and intentions of threat actors, focusing on the human element in cyber threats.

Question: How does the kill chain framework assist organizations in proactive defense?

a) By providing a high-level view of geopolitical factors

b) By aligning defenses with each stage of the cyber attack process

c) By analyzing specific attack tactics

d) By focusing on day-to-day threat responses

Answer: b) By aligning defenses with each stage of the cyber attack process

Explanation: The kill chain framework helps organizations align defenses with each stage of a cyber attack, enabling proactive defense strategies.

Question: What is the primary goal of reverse engineering in threat research?

a) To analyze specific attack tactics

b) To dissect malware and understand its inner workings

c) To focus on day-to-day threat responses

d) To provide a high-level view of geopolitical factors

Answer: b) To dissect malware and understand its inner workings

Explanation: Reverse engineering involves dissecting malware to understand its functionality, vulnerabilities, and potential countermeasures.

Question: How does the STRIDE model contribute to threat modeling?

a) By analyzing specific attack tactics

b) By focusing on day-to-day threat responses

c) By providing insights into human-centric aspects of threat actors

d) By categorizing threats based on Spoofing, Tampering, Repudiation, Information Disclosure, Denial of Service, and Elevation of Privilege

Answer: d) By categorizing threats based on Spoofing, Tampering, Repudiation, Information Disclosure, Denial of Service, and Elevation of Privilege

Explanation: The STRIDE model categorizes threats based on six dimensions, aiding in systematic threat modeling.

Question: How does the DREAD model assist in prioritizing security measures?

a) By analyzing specific attack tactics

b) By providing a high-level view of geopolitical factors

c) By assessing potential impact and likelihood of threats based on Damage, Reproducibility, Exploitability, Affected Users, and Discoverability

d) By focusing on day-to-day threat responses

Answer: c) By assessing potential impact and likelihood of threats based on Damage, Reproducibility, Exploitability, Affected Users, and Discoverability

Explanation: The DREAD model helps prioritize security measures by assessing the potential impact and likelihood of threats.

Question: How do Information Sharing and Analysis Centers (ISACs) contribute to threat intelligence?

a) By dissecting malware and understanding its inner workings

b) By focusing on day-to-day threat responses

c) By serving as collaborative platforms for organizations to share threat intelligence

d) By providing a high-level view of geopolitical factors

Answer: c) By serving as collaborative platforms for organizations to share threat intelligence

Explanation: ISACs facilitate the sharing of threat intelligence among organizations within specific industries.

Question: In threat intelligence, what is the main focus of tactical intelligence?

a) Long-term security strategies

b) Current threats and day-to-day responses

c) Universal language for describing threats

d) Geopolitical factors influencing cyber threats

Answer: b) Current threats and day-to-day responses

Explanation: Tactical intelligence focuses on specific details related to current threats, aiding in day-to-day threat responses.

Question: How does technical intelligence (TechINT) contribute to cybersecurity defense?

a) By providing a high-level view of geopolitical factors

b) By analyzing specific attack tactics

c) By delving into the technical details of threats, including malware and vulnerabilities

d) By aligning defenses with each stage of the cyber attack process

Answer: c) By delving into the technical details of threats, including malware and vulnerabilities

Explanation: TechINT provides in-depth technical details to identify and counter specific technical aspects of threats.

Question: What is the significance of the MITRE ATT&CK framework in threat intelligence?

a) It focuses on day-to-day threat responses

b) It serves as a universal language for describing cyber threats

c) It analyzes specific attack tactics

d) It provides insights into long-term security strategies

Answer: b) It serves as a universal language for describing cyber threats

Explanation: The MITRE ATT&CK framework serves as a universal language for describing cyber threats, aiding in threat intelligence sharing and analysis.

Question: How does operational intelligence contribute to cybersecurity?

a) By providing insights into long-term trends

b) By analyzing specific attack tactics

c) By addressing day-to-day threats and responses

d) By focusing on geopolitical factors influencing cyber threats

Answer: c) By addressing day-to-day threats and responses

Explanation: Operational intelligence focuses on current threats and aids in day-to-day threat responses.

Question: What perspective does the Diamond Model of Intrusion Analysis emphasize?

a) Geopolitical factors influencing cyber threats

b) The Adversary, Infrastructure, Capability, and Victim perspectives

c) Analyzing specific attack tactics

d) Providing a high-level view of cybersecurity threats

Answer: b) The Adversary, Infrastructure, Capability, and Victim perspectives

Explanation: The Diamond Model emphasizes the analysis of the Adversary, Infrastructure, Capability, and Victim perspectives.

Question: How does reverse engineering contribute to threat research?

a) By dissecting malware and understanding its inner workings

b) By providing a high-level view of geopolitical factors

c) By analyzing specific attack tactics

d) By addressing day-to-day threats and responses

Answer: a) By dissecting malware and understanding its inner workings

Explanation: Reverse engineering involves dissecting malware to understand its functionality, vulnerabilities, and potential countermeasures.

Question: What is the primary goal of the kill chain framework?

a) To provide a high-level view of geopolitical factors

b) To align defenses with each stage of the cyber attack process

c) To analyze specific attack tactics

d) To focus on long-term security strategies

Answer: b) To align defenses with each stage of the cyber attack process

Explanation: The kill chain framework helps align defenses with each stage of a cyber attack, enabling proactive defense strategies.

Question: How does human intelligence (HumINT) differ from technical intelligence (TechINT)?

a) HumINT focuses on human-centric aspects of threat actors, while TechINT delves into technical details of threats

b) HumINT analyzes malware and vulnerabilities, while TechINT provides insights into motivations of threat actors

c) Both HumINT and TechINT focus on day-to-day threat responses

d) Both HumINT and TechINT provide a high-level view of cybersecurity threats

Answer: a) HumINT focuses on human-centric aspects of threat actors, while TechINT delves into technical details of threats

Explanation: HumINT focuses on the human element in cyber threats, while TechINT provides technical details of threats.

Question: How does the STRIDE model aid in systematic threat modeling?

a) By analyzing specific attack tactics

b) By dissecting malware and understanding its inner workings

c) By providing insights into human-centric aspects of threat actors

d) By categorizing threats based on Spoofing, Tampering, Repudiation, Information Disclosure, Denial of Service, and Elevation of Privilege

Answer: d) By categorizing threats based on Spoofing, Tampering, Repudiation, Information Disclosure, Denial of Service, and Elevation of Privilege

Explanation: The STRIDE model categorizes threats based on six dimensions, aiding in systematic threat modeling.

Question: What is the primary focus of tactical intelligence in threat intelligence?

a) Long-term security strategies

b) Current threats and day-to-day responses

c) Universal language for describing threats

d) Geopolitical factors influencing cyber threats

Answer: b) Current threats and day-to-day responses

Explanation: Tactical intelligence focuses on specific details related to current threats, aiding in day-to-day threat responses.

Question: How does technical intelligence (TechINT) contribute to cybersecurity defense?

a) By providing a high-level view of geopolitical factors

b) By analyzing specific attack tactics

c) By delving into the technical details of threats, including malware and vulnerabilities

d) By aligning defenses with each stage of the cyber attack process

Answer: c) By delving into the technical details of threats, including malware and vulnerabilities

Explanation: TechINT provides in-depth technical details to identify and counter specific technical aspects of threats.

Question: What is the significance of the MITRE ATT&CK framework in threat intelligence?

a) It focuses on day-to-day threat responses

b) It serves as a universal language for describing cyber threats

c) It analyzes specific attack tactics

d) It provides insights into long-term security strategies

Answer: b) It serves as a universal language for describing cyber threats

Explanation: The MITRE ATT&CK framework serves as a universal language for describing cyber threats, aiding in threat intelligence sharing and analysis.

Question: How does operational intelligence contribute to cybersecurity?

a) By providing insights into long-term trends

b) By analyzing specific attack tactics

c) By addressing day-to-day threats and responses

d) By focusing on geopolitical factors influencing cyber threats

Answer: c) By addressing day-to-day threats and responses

Explanation: Operational intelligence focuses on current threats and aids in day-to-day threat responses.

Question: What perspective does the Diamond Model of Intrusion Analysis emphasize?

a) Geopolitical factors influencing cyber threats

b) The Adversary, Infrastructure, Capability, and Victim perspectives

c) Analyzing specific attack tactics

d) Providing a high-level view of cybersecurity threats

Answer: b) The Adversary, Infrastructure, Capability, and Victim perspectives

Explanation: The Diamond Model emphasizes the analysis of the Adversary, Infrastructure, Capability, and Victim perspectives.

Question: How does reverse engineering contribute to threat research?

a) By dissecting malware and understanding its inner workings

b) By providing a high-level view of geopolitical factors

c) By analyzing specific attack tactics

d) By addressing day-to-day threats and responses

Answer: a) By dissecting malware and understanding its inner workings

Explanation: Reverse engineering involves dissecting malware to understand its functionality, vulnerabilities, and potential countermeasures.

Question: What is the primary goal of the kill chain framework?

a) To provide a high-level view of geopolitical factors

b) To align defenses with each stage of the cyber attack process

c) To analyze specific attack tactics

d) To focus on long-term security strategies

Answer: b) To align defenses with each stage of the cyber attack process

Explanation: The kill chain framework helps align defenses with each stage of a cyber attack, enabling proactive defense strategies.

Question: How does human intelligence (HumINT) differ from technical intelligence (TechINT)?

a) HumINT focuses on human-centric aspects of threat actors, while TechINT delves into technical details of threats

b) HumINT analyzes malware and vulnerabilities, while TechINT provides insights into motivations of threat actors

c) Both HumINT and TechINT focus on day-to-day threat responses

d) Both HumINT and TechINT provide a high-level view of cybersecurity threats

Answer: a) HumINT focuses on human-centric aspects of threat actors, while TechINT delves into technical details of threats

Explanation: HumINT focuses on the human element in cyber threats, while TechINT provides technical details of threats.

Question: How does the STRIDE model aid in systematic threat modeling?

a) By analyzing specific attack tactics

b) By dissecting malware and understanding its inner workings

c) By providing insights into human-centric aspects of threat actors

d) By categorizing threats based on Spoofing, Tampering, Repudiation, Information Disclosure, Denial of Service, and Elevation of Privilege

Answer: d) By categorizing threats based on Spoofing, Tampering, Repudiation, Information Disclosure, Denial of Service, and Elevation of Privilege

Explanation: The STRIDE model categorizes threats based on six dimensions, aiding in systematic threat modeling.

Question: What is the primary focus of tactical intelligence in threat intelligence?

a) Long-term security strategies

b) Current threats and day-to-day responses

c) Universal language for describing threats

d) Geopolitical factors influencing cyber threats

Answer: b) Current threats and day-to-day responses

Explanation: Tactical intelligence focuses on specific details related to current threats, aiding in day-to-day threat responses.

Question: How does technical intelligence (TechINT) contribute to cybersecurity defense?

a) By providing a high-level view of geopolitical factors

b) By analyzing specific attack tactics

c) By delving into the technical details of threats, including malware and vulnerabilities

d) By aligning defenses with each stage of the cyber attack process

Answer: c) By delving into the technical details of threats, including malware and vulnerabilities

Explanation: TechINT provides in-depth technical details to identify and counter specific technical aspects of threats.

Chapter 3: Vulnerability Management Activities

In the relentless pursuit of a robust cybersecurity posture, effective vulnerability management is paramount. This chapter delves into the critical activities surrounding vulnerability identification, providing insights into the methodologies and tools essential for identifying and cataloging vulnerabilities within an organizational environment.

Continuous Monitoring:

Methodology: Implementing continuous monitoring mechanisms to detect vulnerabilities in real-time.

Significance: Continuous monitoring ensures that new vulnerabilities are promptly identified, allowing organizations to stay proactive in their response efforts.

Automated Vulnerability Scanning:

Methodology: Utilizing automated tools to scan networks, systems, and applications for known vulnerabilities.

Significance: Automated scanning accelerates the identification process, providing a comprehensive overview of vulnerabilities across the IT landscape.

Asset Inventory Management:

Methodology: Maintaining an up-to-date inventory of organizational assets, including hardware, software, and configurations.

Significance: A comprehensive asset inventory aids in pinpointing vulnerabilities associated with specific systems, facilitating targeted remediation.

Patch Management Integration:

Methodology: Integrating vulnerability identification with patch management processes to streamline the remediation lifecycle.

Significance: Aligning vulnerability identification with patch management ensures a synchronized approach to addressing identified vulnerabilities promptly.

Collaborative Threat Intelligence:

Methodology: Leveraging threat intelligence sources to identify vulnerabilities targeted by current cyber threats.

Significance: Collaborative threat intelligence enhances the accuracy of vulnerability identification by aligning it with the latest threat landscape.

Scanning Parameters and Criteria:

As organizations navigate the intricate landscape of vulnerability scanning, understanding the parameters and criteria governing the scanning process is pivotal. This section dissects the essential elements that shape vulnerability scanning activities, ensuring a targeted and effective approach to identifying and mitigating vulnerabilities.

Scope Definition:

Parameters: Defining the scope of the vulnerability scanning process, including specific networks, systems, or applications to be assessed.

Criteria: Ensuring that the scope aligns with organizational priorities and risk management objectives.

Comprehensive Asset Coverage:

Parameters: Ensuring that vulnerability scanning covers the entire spectrum of organizational assets.

Criteria: Verifying that all critical assets, including servers, endpoints, and network devices, undergo thorough scanning to minimize blind spots.

Frequency and Timing:

Parameters: Establishing the frequency and timing of vulnerability scans based on organizational needs and operational considerations.

Criteria: Adapting the scanning schedule to accommodate system uptime requirements and minimize disruptions to critical business processes.

Credential-based Scanning:

Parameters: Utilizing credentials to conduct authenticated scans, providing a deeper assessment of vulnerabilities.

Criteria: Ensuring that credential-based scanning is employed where feasible, enhancing the accuracy of vulnerability identification.

Customized Vulnerability Databases:

Parameters: Tailoring vulnerability databases to align with organizational technology stacks and software applications.

Criteria: Verifying that the vulnerability database used for scanning reflects the specific technologies deployed within the organization for precise identification.

Severity Prioritization:

Parameters: Assigning severity levels to identified vulnerabilities based on their potential impact.

Criteria: Developing a prioritization framework that considers business-critical systems and potential exploitability, guiding remediation efforts effectively.

Regulatory Compliance Mapping:

Parameters: Mapping vulnerability scanning criteria to regulatory compliance requirements.

Criteria: Ensuring that vulnerability scanning aligns with regulatory mandates, providing a proactive stance toward compliance adherence.

By unraveling the intricacies of vulnerability identification and establishing clear parameters for scanning activities, organizations can fortify their defenses against potential threats. This chapter equips cybersecurity practitioners with the knowledge needed to conduct targeted vulnerability management activities, fostering a proactive security posture.

Intrusion Prevention System (IPS):

In the ever-evolving landscape of cybersecurity, an Intrusion Prevention System (IPS) plays a pivotal role in safeguarding organizational networks. This chapter explores the functionalities, deployment strategies, and optimization techniques for IPS, providing a comprehensive understanding of its role in proactive threat mitigation.

IPS Functionality Overview:

Description: Delving into the core functionalities of an IPS, including real-time threat detection, analysis, and automated response mechanisms.

Significance: Understanding how an IPS actively prevents and mitigates security threats, including malicious activities and network-based attacks.

Deployment Strategies:

In-line Deployment: Examining the advantages and considerations of deploying an IPS in-line with network traffic for real-time threat prevention.

Out-of-Band Deployment: Exploring the benefits of out-of-band deployment, allowing for threat analysis without impacting live network traffic.

Tuning and Optimization:

Signature Updates: Addressing the importance of timely signature updates to ensure the IPS remains effective against emerging threats.

False Positive Mitigation: Implementing strategies to reduce false positives and enhance the accuracy of threat detection.

Intrusion Detection System (IDS):

In the intricate dance between defenders and adversaries, an Intrusion Detection System (IDS) serves as a vigilant sentinel, detecting and alerting to potential threats. This section navigates through the nuances of IDS, covering its operational principles, alert mechanisms, and integration into a comprehensive security architecture.

Operational Principles:

Signature-Based Detection: Exploring how signature-based detection mechanisms identify known patterns of malicious activity.

Anomaly-Based Detection: Unraveling the concept of anomaly-based detection, which identifies deviations from normal network behavior.

Alert Mechanisms:

Alert Prioritization: Establishing a framework for prioritizing alerts based on severity, impact, and potential risk.

Notification and Response: Defining protocols for timely notification and response to IDS alerts, minimizing the dwell time of potential threats.

Integration with Security Architecture:

SIEM Integration: Understanding the synergy between IDS and Security Information and Event Management (SIEM) systems for centralized log analysis and correlation.

Collaboration with Firewalls: Exploring how IDS collaborates with firewalls to create a layered defense, enhancing the overall security posture.

Firewall Settings:

As the first line of defense, firewalls act as gatekeepers, regulating incoming and outgoing network traffic. This segment dissects firewall settings, covering configuration best practices, rule management, and the application of security policies to fortify network perimeters.

Configuration Best Practices:

Default Deny Policy: Advocating for a default deny policy to restrict all traffic by default, allowing only explicitly permitted communications.

Rule Logging: Emphasizing the importance of rule logging to track and analyze firewall activities for potential security incidents.

Rule Management:

Rule Prioritization: Establishing a systematic approach to prioritizing firewall rules based on security requirements.

Regular Rule Review: Encouraging periodic reviews and updates of firewall rules to align with evolving organizational needs and security threats.

Application of Security Policies:

Segmentation Policies: Implementing network segmentation policies to isolate and contain potential threats, limiting lateral movement.

User-Based Policies: Integrating user-based policies into firewalls to enforce granular access controls based on user roles and responsibilities.

Generating Reports:

In the quest for comprehensive network visibility, generating insightful reports becomes paramount. This chapter elucidates the art of report generation, covering the types of reports, key metrics, and the strategic use of reporting tools for informed decision-making.

Types of Reports:

Incident Reports: Crafting reports detailing security incidents, including the nature of the incident, response actions taken, and lessons learned.

Compliance Reports: Generating reports aligned with regulatory and compliance requirements to demonstrate adherence to security standards.

Key Metrics for Analysis:

Incident Trends: Analyzing trends in security incidents over time to identify recurrent patterns and potential areas for improvement.

Response Effectiveness: Evaluating the effectiveness of incident response efforts through metrics such as response time and containment success.

Validation:

In the dynamic realm of cybersecurity, validation serves as the litmus test for the efficacy of defense mechanisms. This section explores the methodologies and practices of validation, ensuring that security measures are not only implemented but also robustly tested.

Penetration Testing:

Simulated Attacks: Conducting controlled and ethical simulated attacks to identify vulnerabilities and assess the resilience of defenses.

Red Team Exercises: Engaging in red team exercises to emulate real-world threat scenarios and evaluate the organization's ability to detect and respond.

Vulnerability Assessments:

Continuous Scanning: Implementing continuous vulnerability scanning to identify and remediate potential weaknesses in the network.

Risk Prioritization: Prioritizing vulnerabilities based on their potential impact and the level of risk they pose to the organization.

Security Posture Evaluation:

Comprehensive Audits: Performing comprehensive security audits to evaluate the overall security posture, including policy adherence and configuration hygiene.

Continuous Improvement Plans: Establishing iterative improvement plans based on validation findings, fostering a culture of continuous enhancement.

This chapter navigates the intricate landscape of network defense strategies, from the proactive capabilities of IPS and IDS to the foundational role of firewalls, the art of generating insightful reports, and the imperative of robust validation practices. By unraveling these layers, organizations can fortify their networks against the dynamic and evolving threat landscape.

Remediation:

In the aftermath of threat detection and vulnerability identification, effective remediation strategies are essential to close security gaps and fortify organizational defenses. This chapter delves into the intricacies of remediation, covering methodologies, prioritization frameworks, and the role of automation in expediting the response to security incidents.

Prioritization Frameworks:

Risk-Based Approach: Implementing a risk-based approach to prioritize remediation efforts based on the potential impact and likelihood of exploitation.

Asset Criticality: Considering the criticality of assets in the prioritization process, ensuring that remediation efforts align with business objectives.

Patch Management Best Practices:

Timely Patching: Emphasizing the importance of timely application of security patches to address known vulnerabilities.

Testing Procedures: Implementing robust testing procedures to ensure that patches do not introduce new issues or disruptions.

Configuration Management:

Baseline Configurations: Establishing and maintaining baseline configurations for systems and applications to reduce the attack surface.

Continuous Monitoring: Enabling continuous monitoring of configurations to detect unauthorized changes promptly.

Automated Remediation:

Scripted Responses: Leveraging scripted responses and automation tools to streamline the remediation process for common and repetitive security issues.

Orchestration Platforms: Implementing orchestration platforms to coordinate and automate complex remediation workflows across diverse systems.

Inhibitors to Remediation:

While the intent is to swiftly address security vulnerabilities, various inhibitors may impede the remediation process. This section navigates through the common obstacles and challenges that organizations encounter during remediation efforts.

Resource Constraints:

Limited Personnel: Addressing challenges arising from a shortage of skilled cybersecurity personnel available for remediation tasks.

Budgetary Constraints: Mitigating resource limitations, including financial constraints that may hinder the acquisition of necessary tools or services.

Complexity of IT Environments:

Diverse Technologies: Managing the complexity associated with diverse IT environments comprising a myriad of technologies, platforms, and applications.

Interdependencies: Navigating the intricate web of interdependencies between systems and applications that complicates the remediation process.

Regulatory Compliance Pressures:

Compliance Deadlines: Balancing the urgency of meeting regulatory compliance deadlines with the need for thorough remediation efforts.

Documentation Requirements: Addressing the time-consuming nature of documenting remediation activities to meet compliance standards.

Organizational Resistance:

Change Management Challenges: Overcoming resistance to change within the organization, particularly when implementing remediation measures that may impact established workflows.

Communication Breakdowns: Mitigating challenges related to communication breakdowns between security teams and other organizational units.

Ongoing Scanning and Continuous Monitoring:

In the dynamic landscape of cybersecurity, ongoing scanning and continuous monitoring are indispensable components of a proactive defense strategy. This section explores the importance of continual vigilance, real-time threat detection, and the iterative nature of security measures.

Continuous Vulnerability Scanning:

Real-Time Identification: Conducting continuous vulnerability scanning to identify new vulnerabilities promptly as they emerge.

Integration with Patching: Ensuring seamless integration with patch management processes for immediate remediation actions.

Behavioral Analytics:

Anomaly Detection: Implementing behavioral analytics to detect anomalous patterns of activity that may indicate security threats.

User Behavior Monitoring: Monitoring user behavior to identify deviations from normal usage patterns that may signal potential security incidents.

Threat Intelligence Integration:

Real-Time Updates: Integrating threat intelligence feeds for real-time updates on emerging threats and evolving attack techniques.

Automated Response: Implementing automated response mechanisms based on threat intelligence to proactively thwart potential threats.

Log Aggregation and Correlation:

Centralized Logging: Aggregating logs from diverse sources into a centralized platform for comprehensive visibility.

Correlation Analysis: Employing correlation analysis to identify patterns and relationships between disparate log entries, aiding in threat detection.

Incident Response Readiness:

Playbook Development: Developing incident response playbooks outlining predefined actions and responses for different types of security incidents.

Regular Drills: Conducting regular incident response drills to ensure the readiness and effectiveness of response teams.

In the pursuit of a resilient cybersecurity posture, the journey doesn't conclude with detection; it extends into the realm of swift and effective remediation. Overcoming inhibitors, embracing ongoing scanning, and maintaining continuous monitoring are integral facets of this journey, fostering an environment where security is not a static state but an evolving, adaptive process.

Practice Questions and Answers

Question: What is the primary purpose of continuous monitoring in vulnerability management?

a) To conduct periodic scans

b) To detect vulnerabilities in real-time

c) To generate compliance reports

d) To prioritize vulnerabilities

Answer: b) To detect vulnerabilities in real-time

Explanation: Continuous monitoring ensures the real-time detection of vulnerabilities, allowing for prompt remediation.

Question: How does automated vulnerability scanning contribute to the vulnerability management process?

a) By conducting manual assessments

b) By identifying vulnerabilities in real-time

c) By generating compliance reports

d) By analyzing threat intelligence

Answer: b) By identifying vulnerabilities in real-time

Explanation: Automated scanning accelerates the identification of vulnerabilities, providing a comprehensive overview of the security landscape.

Question: Why is asset inventory management crucial in vulnerability management?

a) To conduct penetration testing

b) To prioritize vulnerabilities based on severity

c) To maintain an up-to-date list of organizational assets

d) To analyze threat intelligence

Answer: c) To maintain an up-to-date list of organizational assets

Explanation: A comprehensive asset inventory aids in pinpointing vulnerabilities associated with specific systems, facilitating targeted remediation.

Question: How does patch management integration enhance vulnerability management?

a) By conducting manual assessments

b) By aligning vulnerability identification with patch management processes

c) By analyzing threat intelligence

d) By generating compliance reports

Answer: b) By aligning vulnerability identification with patch management processes

Explanation: Integration with patch management ensures a synchronized approach to addressing identified vulnerabilities promptly.

Question: What is the significance of collaborative threat intelligence in vulnerability management?

a) To conduct penetration testing

b) To generate compliance reports

c) To prioritize vulnerabilities based on severity

d) To align vulnerability management with business objectives

Answer: c) To prioritize vulnerabilities based on severity

Explanation: Collaborative threat intelligence enhances the accuracy of vulnerability identification by aligning it with the latest threat landscape.

Question: In vulnerability scanning, what does the scope definition involve?

a) Defining the severity of vulnerabilities

b) Defining the frequency of scanning

c) Defining the specific networks, systems, or applications to be assessed

d) Defining the compliance requirements

Answer: c) Defining the specific networks, systems, or applications to be assessed

Explanation: Scope definition involves specifying the areas to be covered during vulnerability scanning.

Question: Why is comprehensive asset coverage important in vulnerability scanning?

a) To conduct manual assessments

b) To prioritize vulnerabilities based on severity

c) To analyze threat intelligence

d) To ensure all critical assets undergo thorough scanning

Answer: d) To ensure all critical assets undergo thorough scanning

Explanation: Comprehensive asset coverage ensures that all critical assets are included in the vulnerability scanning process.

Question: What role does credential-based scanning play in vulnerability management?

a) To generate compliance reports

b) To prioritize vulnerabilities based on severity

c) To conduct manual assessments

d) To conduct authenticated scans for a deeper assessment

Answer: d) To conduct authenticated scans for a deeper assessment

Explanation: Credential-based scanning provides a deeper assessment of vulnerabilities by conducting authenticated scans.

Question: How does customized vulnerability databases contribute to vulnerability scanning?

a) By conducting manual assessments

b) By aligning vulnerability scanning with regulatory compliance

c) By tailoring databases to organizational technology stacks

d) By analyzing threat intelligence

Answer: c) By tailoring databases to organizational technology stacks

Explanation: Customized vulnerability databases reflect the specific technologies deployed within the organization, aiding in precise identification.

Question: Why is severity prioritization essential in vulnerability management?

a) To generate compliance reports

b) To conduct penetration testing

c) To assess the impact and prioritize remediation efforts

d) To align vulnerability management with business objectives

Answer: c) To assess the impact and prioritize remediation efforts

Explanation: Severity prioritization helps in focusing remediation efforts on vulnerabilities with the highest potential impact.

Question: What is the primary purpose of continuous vulnerability scanning?

a) To conduct manual assessments

b) To align vulnerability scanning with patch management

c) To detect vulnerabilities in real-time

d) To generate compliance reports

Answer: c) To detect vulnerabilities in real-time

Explanation: Continuous vulnerability scanning ensures the real-time detection of vulnerabilities for prompt remediation.

Question: How does behavioral analytics contribute to ongoing vulnerability management?

a) By prioritizing vulnerabilities based on severity

b) By conducting manual assessments

c) By detecting anomalous patterns of activity

d) By analyzing threat intelligence

Answer: c) By detecting anomalous patterns of activity

Explanation: Behavioral analytics aids in detecting deviations from normal behavior, signaling potential security threats.

Question: Why is integration with threat intelligence important in ongoing vulnerability management?

a) To conduct penetration testing

b) To generate compliance reports

c) To align vulnerability scanning with patch management

d) To receive real-time updates on emerging threats

Answer: d) To receive real-time updates on emerging threats

Explanation: Integration with threat intelligence provides real-time updates on emerging threats, enhancing proactive threat mitigation.

Question: What is the role of automated response mechanisms in ongoing vulnerability management?

a) To generate compliance reports

b) To conduct manual assessments

c) To streamline the remediation process for common issues

d) To prioritize vulnerabilities based on severity

Answer: c) To streamline the remediation process for common issues

Explanation: Automated response mechanisms streamline the remediation process for common and repetitive security issues.

Question: How does log aggregation contribute to continuous monitoring in vulnerability management?

a) By conducting manual assessments

b) By generating compliance reports

c) By aggregating logs for comprehensive visibility

d) By aligning vulnerability scanning with patch management

Answer: c) By aggregating logs for comprehensive visibility

Explanation: Log aggregation provides comprehensive visibility into activities, aiding in continuous monitoring.

Question: What is the purpose of incident response playbooks in ongoing vulnerability management?

a) To generate compliance reports

b) To conduct manual assessments

c) To streamline the incident response process

d) To prioritize vulnerabilities based on severity

Answer: c) To streamline the incident response process

Explanation: Incident response playbooks outline predefined actions and responses, streamlining the incident response process.

Question: How does penetration testing contribute to ongoing vulnerability management?

a) By prioritizing vulnerabilities based on severity

b) By conducting simulated attacks to identify weaknesses

c) By aligning vulnerability scanning with patch management

d) By generating compliance reports

Answer: b) By conducting simulated attacks to identify weaknesses

Explanation: Penetration testing involves controlled simulated attacks to identify vulnerabilities and weaknesses.

Question: What role does vulnerability assessment play in ongoing vulnerability management?

a) By aligning vulnerability scanning with patch management

b) By prioritizing vulnerabilities based on severity

c) By conducting continuous scanning to identify weaknesses

d) By generating compliance reports

Answer: c) By conducting continuous scanning to identify weaknesses

Explanation: Vulnerability assessment involves continuous scanning to identify and remediate weaknesses in the network.

Question: How does risk prioritization aid in ongoing vulnerability management?

a) By generating compliance reports

b) By aligning vulnerability scanning with patch management

c) By conducting manual assessments

d) By prioritizing vulnerabilities based on potential impact

Answer: d) By prioritizing vulnerabilities based on potential impact

Explanation: Risk prioritization helps in focusing remediation efforts on vulnerabilities with the highest potential impact.

Question: Why is comprehensive audit important in ongoing vulnerability management?

a) To conduct penetration testing

b) To generate compliance reports

c) To align vulnerability scanning with patch management

d) To evaluate the overall security posture

Answer: d) To evaluate the overall security posture

Explanation: Comprehensive audits evaluate the overall security posture, including policy adherence and configuration hygiene.

Question: How does orchestration platforms contribute to ongoing vulnerability management?

a) By conducting manual assessments

b) By streamlining the remediation process through automation

c) By aligning vulnerability scanning with patch management

d) By generating compliance reports

Answer: b) By streamlining the remediation process through automation

Explanation: Orchestration platforms coordinate and automate complex remediation workflows.

Question: What is the primary purpose of behavioral analytics in vulnerability management?

a) To prioritize vulnerabilities based on severity

b) To conduct manual assessments

c) To detect anomalous patterns of activity

d) To generate compliance reports

Answer: c) To detect anomalous patterns of activity

Explanation: Behavioral analytics aids in detecting deviations from normal behavior, signaling potential security threats.

Question: How does log correlation analysis contribute to continuous monitoring in vulnerability management?

a) By generating compliance reports

b) By conducting manual assessments

c) By aggregating logs for comprehensive visibility

d) By aligning vulnerability scanning with patch management

Answer: c) By aggregating logs for comprehensive visibility

Explanation: Log correlation analysis identifies patterns and relationships between disparate log entries, aiding in continuous monitoring.

Question: Why is risk prioritization crucial in ongoing vulnerability management?

a) To conduct penetration testing

b) To align vulnerability scanning with patch management

c) To assess the impact and prioritize remediation efforts

d) To generate compliance reports

Answer: c) To assess the impact and prioritize remediation efforts

Explanation: Risk prioritization helps in focusing remediation efforts on vulnerabilities with the highest potential impact.

Question: How does real-time vulnerability scanning contribute to ongoing vulnerability management?

a) By conducting manual assessments

b) By aligning vulnerability scanning with patch management

c) By detecting vulnerabilities promptly as they emerge

d) By generating compliance reports

Answer: c) By detecting vulnerabilities promptly as they emerge

Explanation: Real-time vulnerability scanning ensures the prompt detection of vulnerabilities for immediate remediation.

Question: What is the role of user behavior monitoring in ongoing vulnerability management?

a) To prioritize vulnerabilities based on severity

b) To conduct manual assessments

c) To detect anomalous patterns of user activity

d) To align vulnerability scanning with patch management

Answer: c) To detect anomalous patterns of user activity

Explanation: User behavior monitoring helps in detecting deviations from normal user activity, signaling potential security threats.

Question: How does real-time integration with threat intelligence contribute to ongoing vulnerability management?

a) By generating compliance reports

b) By aligning vulnerability scanning with patch management

c) By receiving real-time updates on emerging threats

d) By conducting manual assessments

Answer: c) By receiving real-time updates on emerging threats

Explanation: Real-time integration with threat intelligence provides timely updates on emerging threats, enhancing proactive threat mitigation.

28. Question: What is the purpose of incident response readiness in ongoing vulnerability management?

css

Copy code

a) To prioritize vulnerabilities based on severity

b) To conduct manual assessments

c) To streamline the incident response process

d) To generate compliance reports

Answer: c) To streamline the incident response process

Explanation: Incident response readiness involves preparing and streamlining the incident response process for effective and swift actions.

29. Question: How does vulnerability scanning contribute to ongoing vulnerability management?

vbnet

Copy code

a) By conducting continuous scanning to identify weaknesses

b) By generating compliance reports

c) By aligning vulnerability scanning with patch management

d) By prioritizing vulnerabilities based on severity

Answer: a) By conducting continuous scanning to identify weaknesses

Explanation: Vulnerability scanning involves continuous scanning to identify and remediate weaknesses in the network.

30. Question: Why is ongoing vulnerability management crucial in the cybersecurity landscape?

vbnet

Copy code

a) To generate compliance reports

b) To conduct penetration testing

c) To continually assess and address security weaknesses

d) To align vulnerability scanning with patch management

Answer: c) To continually assess and address security weaknesses

Explanation: Ongoing vulnerability management is essential for continuously assessing and addressing security weaknesses to maintain a robust cybersecurity posture.

Chapter 4: Vulnerability Assessment Tools

In the relentless pursuit of a resilient cybersecurity posture, the arsenal of vulnerability assessment tools becomes paramount. This chapter delves into the diverse array of tools designed to identify and mitigate vulnerabilities across different facets of an organization's digital landscape.

Vulnerability Assessment Tools:

Definition: Unraveling the essence of vulnerability assessment as a proactive process to identify, classify, and prioritize security vulnerabilities.

Objective: Understanding how vulnerability assessment contributes to the overall cybersecurity strategy.

Types of Vulnerability Assessment Tools:

Network Scanners: Delving into tools that scrutinize network infrastructure to identify vulnerabilities in routers, switches, and other devices.

Web Application Scanners: Exploring tools designed specifically for assessing vulnerabilities within web applications.

Software Composition Analysis (SCA) Tools: Examining tools that focus on identifying vulnerabilities in third-party and open-source software components.

Database Scanners: Discussing tools tailored for the identification of vulnerabilities within database systems.

Selection Criteria for Vulnerability Assessment Tools:

Scalability: Evaluating tools based on their scalability to accommodate the size and complexity of organizational networks.

Accuracy: Prioritizing tools that provide accurate and reliable vulnerability detection results.

Ease of Use: Assessing the user-friendliness of tools to enhance their adoption and integration into existing workflows.

Reporting Capabilities: Exploring the reporting features of tools to ensure comprehensive and actionable vulnerability reports.

Web Application Scanners:

Role of Web Application Scanners:

Definition: Clarifying the role of web application scanners in identifying security vulnerabilities within web-based software.

Significance: Understanding how web application scanners contribute to the protection of sensitive data and prevention of web-based attacks.

Common Features of Web Application Scanners:

Crawling and Discovery: Exploring how scanners traverse through web applications to identify and map the attack surface.

Automated Testing: Understanding the automated testing capabilities of scanners to identify common vulnerabilities such as SQL injection and cross-site scripting (XSS).

Authentication Testing: Examining how scanners assess the security of authentication mechanisms within web applications.

Reporting and Analysis: Assessing the reporting and analysis features to provide actionable insights for remediation.

Popular Web Application Scanners:

Burp Suite: Analyzing the capabilities of Burp Suite as a comprehensive web application security testing tool.

OWASP ZAP (Zed Attack Proxy): Exploring the open-source nature of OWASP ZAP and its emphasis on automated scanning and testing.

Acunetix: Evaluating Acunetix as a vulnerability scanner known for its robust web application security testing capabilities.

Infrastructure Vulnerability Scanners:

Scope of Infrastructure Vulnerability Scanners:

Definition: Clarifying the focus of infrastructure vulnerability scanners on identifying weaknesses in network devices, operating systems, and services.

Coverage: Exploring the range of assets and components within the IT infrastructure that these scanners assess.

Key Capabilities of Infrastructure Vulnerability Scanners:

Network Discovery: Assessing how scanners identify and catalog devices within the network.

Port and Service Enumeration: Examining the capability of scanners to enumerate open ports and services.

Operating System Fingerprinting: Understanding how scanners determine the underlying operating systems of devices.

Vulnerability Identification: Analyzing the process by which scanners pinpoint vulnerabilities in network devices and systems.

Prominent Infrastructure Vulnerability Scanners:

Nessus: Evaluating Nessus as a widely used vulnerability scanner known for its extensive plugin database.

OpenVAS: Exploring the open-source nature of OpenVAS and its capabilities in network vulnerability scanning.

Qualys Vulnerability Management: Assessing Qualys as a cloud-based vulnerability management solution offering scalability and continuous monitoring.

Software Assessment Tools and Techniques:

Software Composition Analysis (SCA) Overview:

Definition: Unraveling the concept of SCA as a process for identifying and managing vulnerabilities in third-party and open-source software components.

Importance: Understanding the critical role of SCA in mitigating risks associated with software supply chain vulnerabilities.

Capabilities of Software Assessment Tools:

Dependency Analysis: Examining how tools analyze dependencies within software components to identify vulnerabilities.

License Compliance: Assessing the ability of tools to monitor and ensure compliance with software licenses.

Real-time Monitoring: Exploring how tools provide real-time monitoring of open-source components for emerging vulnerabilities.

Integration with Development Workflow: Understanding how these tools seamlessly integrate with the software development lifecycle.

Examples of Software Assessment Tools:

Snyk: Evaluating Snyk as a popular SCA tool known for its real-time monitoring and vulnerability detection capabilities.

Black Duck (Synopsys): Analyzing Black Duck as a comprehensive solution for managing open-source security and license compliance.

WhiteSource: Exploring WhiteSource as a platform that offers continuous security and compliance for open-source components.

In the landscape of vulnerability assessment, a nuanced understanding of the available tools is indispensable. This chapter provides insights into the diverse categories of vulnerability assessment tools, their functionalities, and examples of popular tools within each category. By navigating through this comprehensive overview, cybersecurity practitioners can make informed decisions in selecting and implementing the most suitable tools for their organizational defense strategies.

In the intricate landscape of cybersecurity, the process of enumeration stands as a critical phase for understanding and assessing the target environment comprehensively. This chapter delves into the diverse set of tools and techniques employed for enumeration across various domains, including network, wireless, and cloud infrastructure.

Enumeration Tools and Techniques:

Network Enumeration Techniques:

DNS Enumeration: Exploring how DNS enumeration reveals information about domain names, IP addresses, and associated records.

SNMP Enumeration: Analyzing the use of SNMP (Simple Network Management Protocol) to gather information about network devices.

LDAP Enumeration: Examining the process of LDAP (Lightweight Directory Access Protocol) enumeration for querying directory services.

NetBIOS Enumeration: Understanding NetBIOS enumeration as a method to extract information from Windows-based systems.

Network Enumeration Tools:

Nmap: Evaluating Nmap as a versatile network scanning tool with capabilities for host discovery and port scanning.

ENUM4linux: Assessing ENUM4linux as a specialized tool for extracting information from Windows machines using NetBIOS.

SNMPwalk: Analyzing SNMPwalk for querying SNMP-enabled devices and retrieving information from their Management Information Bases (MIBs).

ldapsearch: Exploring ldapsearch as a command-line tool for querying LDAP directories.

Wireless Assessment Tools:

Aircrack-ng Suite: Evaluating Aircrack-ng as a comprehensive suite for wireless security assessment, including packet capturing and WPA/WPA2 cracking.

Kismet: Analyzing Kismet as a wireless network detector, sniffer, and intrusion detection system.

Wireshark: Exploring Wireshark for wireless packet analysis and capturing, providing insights into network behavior.

Reaver: Assessing Reaver as a tool for brute-force attacks against Wi-Fi Protected Setup (WPS) to retrieve WPA/WPA2 pre-shared keys.

Wireless Enumeration Techniques:

SSID Enumeration: Examining the process of identifying and discovering Service Set Identifiers (SSIDs) within wireless networks.

MAC Address Enumeration: Understanding how MAC addresses can be enumerated to identify connected devices.

Channel Enumeration: Analyzing the enumeration of Wi-Fi channels to understand the distribution of networks in the vicinity.

Probe Request Enumeration: Exploring the use of probe requests to enumerate devices actively searching for Wi-Fi networks.

Cloud Infrastructure Assessment Tools:

AWS CLI (Command Line Interface): Evaluating AWS CLI as a versatile tool for interacting with and assessing Amazon Web Services (AWS) environments.

Azure CLI: Assessing Azure CLI for managing and assessing Microsoft Azure cloud resources.

Terraform: Exploring Terraform as an infrastructure as code (IaC) tool for provisioning and assessing cloud resources across multiple providers.

CloudSploit: Analyzing CloudSploit as a security and compliance scanning tool specifically designed for cloud environments.

Cloud Enumeration Techniques:

Service Enumeration: Examining the identification and enumeration of various cloud services deployed within a cloud environment.

User Enumeration: Understanding the process of enumerating user accounts and permissions within cloud platforms.

Storage Enumeration: Analyzing techniques for enumerating storage resources, including buckets and containers.

Network Enumeration: Exploring the identification and enumeration of network configurations and settings in cloud environments.

Enumeration Best Practices:

Ethical Considerations: Emphasizing the importance of ethical enumeration practices to avoid unnecessary disruptions or harm.

Documentation: Advocating for comprehensive documentation of enumeration activities, findings, and methodologies.

Continuous Monitoring: Highlighting the need for continuous monitoring to detect and respond to potential enumeration attempts.

By navigating through the tools and techniques associated with enumeration in network, wireless, and cloud environments, this chapter equips cybersecurity professionals with the knowledge and skills necessary to conduct thorough assessments. Enumeration, when performed ethically and with careful consideration, becomes a powerful means to fortify defenses, identify vulnerabilities, and enhance the overall security posture in the ever-evolving landscape of cybersecurity.

Practice Questions and Answers

Question: Which type of vulnerability assessment tool is specifically designed to assess weaknesses in third-party and open-source software components?

a) Network Scanners

b) Web Application Scanners

c) Software Composition Analysis (SCA) Tools

d) Database Scanners

Answer: c) Software Composition Analysis (SCA) Tools

Explanation: SCA tools focus on identifying vulnerabilities in third-party and open-source software components.

Question: What is the primary role of web application scanners in the context of vulnerability assessment?

a) Assessing weaknesses in network infrastructure

b) Identifying vulnerabilities within web-based software

c) Enumerating open ports and services

d) Analyzing software licenses

Answer: b) Identifying vulnerabilities within web-based software

Explanation: Web application scanners are designed to assess vulnerabilities specific to web applications.

Question: Which vulnerability assessment tool is known for its extensive plugin database and widely used for network scanning?

a) Nessus

b) OpenVAS

c) Qualys Vulnerability Management

d) Burp Suite

Answer: a) Nessus

Explanation: Nessus is renowned for its extensive plugin database and is widely used for network scanning.

Question: In infrastructure vulnerability scanning, what is the primary function of network discovery?

a) Enumerating open ports and services

b) Identifying vulnerabilities in routers and switches

c) Assessing the security of authentication mechanisms

d) Cataloging devices within the network

Answer: d) Cataloging devices within the network

Explanation: Network discovery involves cataloging devices within the network.

Question: Which wireless assessment tool is known for packet capturing, WPA/WPA2 cracking, and overall wireless security assessment?

a) Wireshark

b) Aircrack-ng Suite

c) Kismet

d) Reaver

Answer: b) Aircrack-ng Suite

Explanation: Aircrack-ng Suite is a comprehensive tool for wireless security assessment, including packet capturing and WPA/WPA2 cracking.

Question: What is the primary purpose of the AWS CLI (Command Line Interface) in cloud infrastructure assessment?

a) Assessing Microsoft Azure cloud resources

b) Managing and assessing Amazon Web Services (AWS) environments

c) Provisioning cloud resources using Terraform

d) Security and compliance scanning for cloud environments

Answer: b) Managing and assessing Amazon Web Services (AWS) environments

Explanation: AWS CLI is used for interacting with and assessing Amazon Web Services (AWS) environments.

Question: Which cloud assessment tool is specifically designed for security and compliance scanning in cloud environments?

a) Terraform

b) CloudSploit

c) Azure CLI

d) AWS CLI

Answer: b) CloudSploit

Explanation: CloudSploit is a security and compliance scanning tool designed for cloud environments.

Question: In network enumeration, what is the role of SNMPwalk?

a) Querying SNMP-enabled devices and retrieving information from MIBs

b) Extracting information from Windows machines using NetBIOS

c) Conducting automated testing for web applications

d) Aggregating logs for comprehensive visibility

Answer: a) Querying SNMP-enabled devices and retrieving information from MIBs

Explanation: SNMPwalk is used for querying SNMP-enabled devices and retrieving information from their Management Information Bases (MIBs).

Question: What is the primary objective of software composition analysis (SCA) tools?

a) Assessing weaknesses in network infrastructure

b) Identifying vulnerabilities in third-party and open-source software components

c) Enumerating open ports and services

d) Analyzing software licenses

Answer: b) Identifying vulnerabilities in third-party and open-source software components

Explanation: SCA tools focus on identifying vulnerabilities in third-party and open-source software components.

Question: Which tool is known for its real-time monitoring and vulnerability detection capabilities in the context of software composition analysis?

a) Black Duck (Synopsys)

b) Snyk

c) WhiteSource

d) Nessus

Answer: b) Snyk

Explanation: Snyk is known for its real-time monitoring and vulnerability detection capabilities in software composition analysis.

Question: In wireless assessment, what does the term "SSID Enumeration" refer to?

a) Identifying and discovering Service Set Identifiers (SSIDs) within wireless networks

b) Enumerating user accounts and permissions within cloud platforms

c) Querying SNMP-enabled devices and retrieving information from MIBs

d) Extracting information from Windows machines using NetBIOS

Answer: a) Identifying and discovering Service Set Identifiers (SSIDs) within wireless networks

Explanation: SSID Enumeration involves identifying and discovering Service Set Identifiers within wireless networks.

Question: What role does Kismet play in wireless security assessment?

a) Conducting brute-force attacks against Wi-Fi Protected Setup (WPS)

b) Capturing and analyzing wireless network packets

c) Analyzing software licenses in open-source components

d) Querying LDAP directories for information

Answer: b) Capturing and analyzing wireless network packets

Explanation: Kismet is a wireless network detector, sniffer, and intrusion detection system for capturing and analyzing wireless network packets.

Question: What is the primary function of Wireshark in the context of wireless assessment?

a) Capturing and analyzing wireless network packets

b) Enumerating open ports and services in network infrastructure

c) Assessing weaknesses in third-party and open-source software components

d) Managing and assessing Amazon Web Services (AWS) environments

Answer: a) Capturing and analyzing wireless network packets

Explanation: Wireshark is used for capturing and analyzing wireless network packets.

Question: How does Terraform contribute to cloud infrastructure assessment?

a) Managing and assessing Amazon Web Services (AWS) environments

b) Interacting with and assessing Microsoft Azure cloud resources

c) Conducting security and compliance scanning in cloud environments

d) Provisioning and managing cloud resources using infrastructure as code (IaC)

Answer: d) Provisioning and managing cloud resources using infrastructure as code (IaC)

Explanation: Terraform is used for provisioning and managing cloud resources using infrastructure as code (IaC).

Question: What is the purpose of continuous monitoring in the context of enumeration?

a) Enumerating open ports and services in network infrastructure

b) Detecting and responding to potential enumeration attempts

c) Capturing and analyzing wireless network packets

d) Identifying vulnerabilities in third-party and open-source software components

Answer: b) Detecting and responding to potential enumeration attempts

Explanation: Continuous monitoring helps in detecting and responding to potential enumeration attempts in real-time.

Question: Which tool is an open-source network scanner widely used for vulnerability assessment and network discovery?

a) Burp Suite

b) OpenVAS

c) OWASP ZAP (Zed Attack Proxy)

d) Acunetix

Answer: b) OpenVAS

Explanation: OpenVAS is an open-source network scanner widely used for vulnerability assessment and network discovery.

Question: What is the primary focus of Nessus as a vulnerability assessment tool?

a) Identifying vulnerabilities in third-party and open-source software components

b) Assessing weaknesses in network infrastructure

c) Analyzing software licenses in open-source components

d) Capturing and analyzing wireless network packets

Answer: b) Assessing weaknesses in network infrastructure

Explanation: Nessus focuses on assessing weaknesses in network infrastructure and is widely used for vulnerability assessment.

Question: Which wireless assessment tool is specifically designed for brute-force attacks against Wi-Fi Protected Setup (WPS)?

a) Wireshark

b) Aircrack-ng Suite

c) Kismet

d) Reaver

Answer: d) Reaver

Explanation: Reaver is a tool designed for brute-force attacks against Wi-Fi Protected Setup (WPS) to retrieve WPA/WPA2 pre-shared keys.

Question: In cloud infrastructure assessment, what is the primary role of CloudSploit?

a) Interacting with and assessing Microsoft Azure cloud resources

b) Managing and assessing Amazon Web Services (AWS) environments

c) Conducting security and compliance scanning in cloud environments

d) Provisioning and managing cloud resources using infrastructure as code (IaC)

Answer: c) Conducting security and compliance scanning in cloud environments

Explanation: CloudSploit is specifically designed for security and compliance scanning in cloud environments.

Question: How does Wireshark contribute to wireless security assessment?

a) Capturing and analyzing wireless network packets

b) Enumerating open ports and services in network infrastructure

c) Assessing weaknesses in third-party and open-source software components

d) Managing and assessing Amazon Web Services (AWS) environments

Answer: a) Capturing and analyzing wireless network packets

Explanation: Wireshark is used for capturing and analyzing wireless network packets.

Question: What is the primary objective of cloud enumeration techniques?

a) Enumerating open ports and services in network infrastructure

b) Identifying vulnerabilities in third-party and open-source software components

c) Assessing weaknesses in routers and switches

d) Identifying and enumerating various cloud services within a cloud environment

Answer: d) Identifying and enumerating various cloud services within a cloud environment

Explanation: Cloud enumeration techniques focus on identifying and enumerating various cloud services within a cloud environment.

Question: What is the role of Aircrack-ng Suite in wireless security assessment?

a) Capturing and analyzing wireless network packets

b) Brute-force attacks against Wi-Fi Protected Setup (WPS)

c) Identifying and discovering Service Set Identifiers (SSIDs) within wireless networks

d) Managing and assessing Amazon Web Services (AWS) environments

Answer: b) Brute-force attacks against Wi-Fi Protected Setup (WPS)

Explanation: Aircrack-ng Suite is known for its capabilities in brute-force attacks against Wi-Fi Protected Setup (WPS).

Question: In software composition analysis, what does the term "Dependency Analysis" refer to?

a) Assessing weaknesses in network infrastructure

b) Analyzing dependencies within software components to identify vulnerabilities

c) Capturing and analyzing wireless network packets

d) Enumerating open ports and services in network infrastructure

Answer: b) Analyzing dependencies within software components to identify vulnerabilities

Explanation: Dependency analysis in software composition analysis involves analyzing dependencies within software components to identify vulnerabilities.

Question: What is the primary purpose of the AWS CLI (Command Line Interface) in cloud infrastructure assessment?

a) Managing and assessing Amazon Web Services (AWS) environments

b) Interacting with and assessing Microsoft Azure cloud resources

c) Conducting security and compliance scanning in cloud environments

d) Provisioning and managing cloud resources using infrastructure as code (IaC)

Answer: a) Managing and assessing Amazon Web Services (AWS) environments

Explanation: AWS CLI is used for managing and assessing Amazon Web Services (AWS) environments.

Question: In network enumeration, what is the role of ENUM4linux?

a) Querying SNMP-enabled devices and retrieving information from MIBs

b) Extracting information from Windows machines using NetBIOS

c) Conducting automated testing for web applications

d) Aggregating logs for comprehensive visibility

Answer: b) Extracting information from Windows machines using NetBIOS

Explanation: ENUM4linux is a tool for extracting information from Windows machines using NetBIOS.

Question: What is the primary focus of Kismet in wireless security assessment?

a) Capturing and analyzing wireless network packets

b) Enumerating open ports and services in network infrastructure

c) Assessing weaknesses in routers and switches

d) Identifying and discovering Service Set Identifiers (SSIDs) within wireless networks

Answer: a) Capturing and analyzing wireless network packets

Explanation: Kismet is a tool for capturing and analyzing wireless network packets.

Question: Which tool is known for its capabilities in real-time monitoring and vulnerability detection in software composition analysis?

a) Black Duck (Synopsys)

b) Snyk

c) WhiteSource

d) Nessus

Answer: b) Snyk

Explanation: Snyk is known for its real-time monitoring and vulnerability detection capabilities in software composition analysis.

Question: What is the primary function of Reaver in wireless security assessment?

a) Capturing and analyzing wireless network packets

b) Brute-force attacks against Wi-Fi Protected Setup (WPS)

c) Identifying and discovering Service Set Identifiers (SSIDs) within wireless networks

d) Managing and assessing Amazon Web Services (AWS) environments

Answer: b) Brute-force attacks against Wi-Fi Protected Setup (WPS)

Explanation: Reaver is designed for brute-force attacks against Wi-Fi Protected Setup (WPS) to retrieve WPA/WPA2 pre-shared keys.

Question: Which tool is an open-source network scanner widely used for vulnerability assessment and network discovery?

a) Burp Suite

b) OpenVAS

c) OWASP ZAP (Zed Attack Proxy)

d) Acunetix

Answer: b) OpenVAS

Explanation: OpenVAS is an open-source network scanner widely used for vulnerability assessment and network discovery.

Question: In infrastructure vulnerability scanning, what is the primary function of operating system fingerprinting?

a) Identifying vulnerabilities in routers and switches

b) Enumerating open ports and services

c) Determining the underlying operating systems of devices

d) Assessing the security of authentication mechanisms

Answer: c) Determining the underlying operating systems of devices

Explanation: Operating system fingerprinting in infrastructure vulnerability scanning involves determining the underlying operating systems of devices.

Chapter 5: Threats and Vulnerabilities Associated with Specialized Technology

In the ever-evolving landscape of cybersecurity, specialized technologies play a pivotal role in shaping the digital ecosystem. This chapter explores the unique threats and vulnerabilities inherent in three key components: access points, virtual private networks (VPNs), mobile devices, and the Internet of Things (IoT).

Access Points:

Introduction to Access Points:

Definition: Unveiling the significance of access points as crucial components in wireless communication.

Functionality: Understanding how access points facilitate connectivity by enabling devices to connect to a wired network wirelessly.

Threats to Access Points:

Wireless Eavesdropping: Analyzing the risk of unauthorized interception of wireless communication.

Rogue Access Points: Exploring the dangers posed by rogue access points that may be set up by malicious actors.

Denial-of-Service (DoS) Attacks: Assessing the impact of DoS attacks on access point availability.

Vulnerabilities in Access Points:

Default Configurations: Examining the risk associated with access points using default configurations.

Outdated Firmware: Discussing the vulnerabilities introduced by access points with outdated firmware.

Lack of Encryption: Analyzing the security implications of access points transmitting data without encryption.

Virtual Private Networks (VPNs):

Overview of VPNs:

Definition: Unraveling the concept of Virtual Private Networks and their role in secure communication over the internet.

Encryption Protocols: Understanding the use of encryption protocols to safeguard data transmitted through VPNs.

Threats to VPNs:

Man-in-the-Middle Attacks: Analyzing the risk of attackers intercepting and altering communication between VPN users.

VPN Endpoint Exploitation: Exploring vulnerabilities in VPN endpoints that can be exploited for unauthorized access.

Protocol Vulnerabilities: Assessing the potential threats associated with vulnerabilities in VPN protocols.

Vulnerabilities in VPNs:

Weak Authentication: Examining the security risks introduced by weak authentication mechanisms in VPNs.

Inadequate Logging: Discussing the importance of comprehensive logging to detect and respond to security incidents.

Insufficient Encryption: Analyzing the vulnerabilities arising from the use of weak encryption algorithms in VPN implementations.

Mobile Devices:

Mobile Device Landscape:

Proliferation of Devices: Understanding the widespread use of mobile devices in personal and professional settings.

Diverse Platforms: Analyzing the security challenges posed by the diversity of mobile operating systems.

Threats to Mobile Devices:

Malware and Ransomware: Examining the risks associated with malicious software targeting mobile platforms.

Unsecured Wi-Fi Networks: Analyzing the threat posed by mobile devices connecting to unsecured Wi-Fi networks.

Device Theft and Loss: Assessing the implications of mobile devices being lost or stolen.

Vulnerabilities in Mobile Devices:

Outdated Software: Discussing the security risks introduced by mobile devices running outdated operating systems.

Insecure Apps: Analyzing the vulnerabilities arising from the installation of unvetted or insecure mobile applications.

Lack of Device Encryption: Examining the security implications of mobile devices lacking proper encryption measures.

Internet of Things (IoT):

Introduction to IoT:

Connected Devices: Understanding the concept of interconnected devices forming the Internet of Things.

Diverse Applications: Analyzing the widespread use of IoT across various industries and sectors.

Threats to IoT:

Insecure Authentication: Examining the risks associated with IoT devices using weak or default authentication mechanisms.

Data Privacy Concerns: Analyzing the threat to user privacy posed by the collection and processing of sensitive data by IoT devices.

Lack of Device Security Updates: Assessing the security risks introduced by IoT devices with no or infrequent security updates.

Vulnerabilities in IoT:

Default Credentials: Discussing the security implications of IoT devices using default or hardcoded credentials.

Inadequate Encryption: Examining vulnerabilities arising from the lack of robust encryption measures in IoT communications.

Insufficient Access Controls: Analyzing the risks associated with IoT devices lacking proper access control mechanisms.

By delving into the threats and vulnerabilities inherent in access points, virtual private networks, mobile devices, and the Internet of Things, this chapter provides cybersecurity practitioners with insights to navigate the challenges posed by these specialized technologies. The understanding of potential risks serves as a foundation for developing effective security strategies in an interconnected and dynamic digital environment.

Embedded Systems:

Foundations of Embedded Systems:

Definition: Unraveling the essence of embedded systems as specialized computing devices integrated into larger systems.

Ubiquity: Understanding the omnipresence of embedded systems in everyday devices and applications.

Threats to Embedded Systems:

Memory Exploitation: Analyzing the risks associated with vulnerabilities in embedded system memory.

Hardware Trojans: Examining the threat posed by clandestine alterations to the hardware design of embedded systems.

Insecure Firmware: Assessing the security implications of vulnerabilities in the firmware controlling embedded systems.

Vulnerabilities in Embedded Systems:

Lack of Security Updates: Discussing the challenges of maintaining security in embedded systems with limited or no update capabilities.

Inadequate Authentication: Analyzing the vulnerabilities introduced by weak or absent authentication mechanisms in embedded devices.

Insufficient Encryption: Examining the security risks arising from the absence of robust encryption in communication protocols.

System on a Chip (SoC):

Overview of System on a Chip:

Definition: Unveiling the concept of System on a Chip as an integrated circuit that encapsulates multiple functions.

Multifunctionality: Understanding the diverse capabilities consolidated into a single chip.

Threats to System on a Chip:

Side-Channel Attacks: Analyzing the risks associated with exploiting unintended information leakage during chip operations.

Counterfeit Components: Examining the threat posed by the infiltration of counterfeit or maliciously altered SoC components.

Hardware Backdoors: Assessing the security implications of undisclosed hardware backdoors in SoC designs.

Vulnerabilities in System on a Chip:

Weak Supply Chain Security: Discussing vulnerabilities introduced through weaknesses in the supply chain processes for SoC components.

Lack of Transparency: Analyzing the challenges associated with the lack of transparency in SoC manufacturing processes.

Insufficient Testing: Examining the security risks arising from inadequate testing of SoC components.

Field Programmable Gate Array (FPGA):

Introduction to Field Programmable Gate Array:

Definition: Unraveling the concept of FPGA as a reconfigurable hardware device.

Customization: Understanding the flexibility of FPGAs for implementing custom logic circuits.

Threats to Field Programmable Gate Array:

Configuration Bitstream Attacks: Analyzing the risks associated with unauthorized access and modification of FPGA configuration bitstreams.

Power Analysis Attacks: Examining the threat posed by analyzing power consumption patterns to extract sensitive information.

Insecure Interfaces: Assessing the security implications of vulnerabilities in communication interfaces of FPGAs.

Vulnerabilities in Field Programmable Gate Array:

Insufficient Access Controls: Discussing the security risks arising from inadequate access controls on FPGA programming interfaces.

Weak Encryption: Analyzing vulnerabilities introduced by the use of weak encryption algorithms in FPGA configurations.

Lack of Runtime Monitoring: Examining the challenges associated with the absence of real-time monitoring capabilities for FPGA configurations.

Physical Access Control:

Essentials of Physical Access Control:

Definition: Unveiling the fundamental concept of physical access control in securing entry points.

Biometric Authentication: Understanding the integration of biometric technologies for enhanced access security.

Threats to Physical Access Control:

Tailgating and Piggybacking: Analyzing the risks associated with unauthorized individuals gaining access by closely following an authorized person.

Biometric Spoofing: Examining the threat posed by attempts to deceive biometric authentication systems.

Insider Threats: Assessing the security implications of authorized personnel exploiting their access for malicious purposes.

Vulnerabilities in Physical Access Control:

Inadequate Monitoring: Discussing vulnerabilities introduced by insufficient surveillance and monitoring of access points.

Single Point of Failure: Analyzing the security risks arising from the reliance on a single access control mechanism.

Lack of Regular Audits: Examining the challenges associated with irregular audits and assessments of physical access control systems.

Connected Vehicles:

Connected Vehicles Landscape:

Definition: Unraveling the concept of connected vehicles as automobiles equipped with internet connectivity and communication capabilities.

Intelligent Transportation Systems (ITS): Understanding the integration of ITS technologies for enhanced vehicle communication.

Threats to Connected Vehicles:

Remote Hacking: Analyzing the risks associated with malicious actors gaining unauthorized access to vehicle systems.

Data Privacy Concerns: Examining the threat to user privacy arising from the collection and processing of vehicle data.

Denial-of-Service (DoS) Attacks: Assessing the impact of DoS attacks on connected vehicle communication.

Vulnerabilities in Connected Vehicles:

Insecure Wireless Communication: Discussing vulnerabilities introduced by the lack of robust encryption in wireless communication between vehicle components.

Lack of Software Updates: Analyzing the security risks arising from the absence of regular and timely software updates in connected vehicles.

Insufficient Authentication: Examining the challenges associated with weak or inadequate authentication mechanisms in connected vehicle systems.

By navigating through the intricacies of embedded systems, System on a Chip, Field Programmable Gate Array, Physical Access Control, and Connected Vehicles, this chapter equips cybersecurity practitioners with the knowledge necessary to address the unique challenges posed by these advanced technologies. Understanding the threats and vulnerabilities in these domains is essential for developing robust security measures in an increasingly interconnected and technologically driven world.

Drones:

Introduction to Drones:

Definition: Unveiling the evolution of unmanned aerial vehicles, commonly known as drones.

Diverse Applications: Understanding the wide-ranging applications of drones in industries such as agriculture, surveillance, and delivery.

Threats to Drones:

Unauthorized Access: Analyzing the risks associated with unauthorized individuals gaining control of drones.

GPS Spoofing: Examining the threat posed by manipulating GPS signals to deceive drone navigation systems.

Data Interception: Assessing the security implications of intercepting data transmitted between drones and ground control stations.

Vulnerabilities in Drones:

Lack of Encryption: Discussing vulnerabilities introduced by the absence of robust encryption in drone communication.

Inadequate Authentication: Analyzing security risks arising from weak or absent authentication mechanisms in drone systems.

Physical Tampering: Examining challenges associated with physical tampering or hijacking of drones.

Industrial Control Systems (ICS):

Foundations of Industrial Control Systems:

Definition: Unraveling the essence of Industrial Control Systems as critical components managing and controlling industrial processes.

Components: Understanding the interconnected components of ICS, including Supervisory Control and Data Acquisition (SCADA) systems.

Threats to Industrial Control Systems:

Cyber Espionage: Analyzing the risks associated with nation-states or threat actors conducting cyber espionage on ICS.

Malware Attacks: Examining the threat posed by malicious software targeting ICS components.

Insider Threats: Assessing the security implications of authorized personnel exploiting their access to compromise ICS.

Vulnerabilities in Industrial Control Systems:

Legacy Systems: Discussing vulnerabilities introduced by the use of outdated and unsupported legacy systems in ICS.

Insecure Communication Protocols: Analyzing security risks arising from the use of insecure communication protocols in ICS networks.

Lack of Network Segmentation: Examining challenges associated with insufficient network segmentation within ICS environments.

SCADA Devices:

Overview of SCADA Devices:

Definition: Unveiling the role of Supervisory Control and Data Acquisition (SCADA) devices in monitoring and controlling industrial processes.

Integration with ICS: Understanding how SCADA devices are integral components of Industrial Control Systems.

Threats to SCADA Devices:

Data Manipulation: Analyzing the risks associated with unauthorized access leading to manipulation of SCADA data.

Physical Attacks: Examining the threat posed by physical attacks on SCADA devices, such as tampering or destruction.

Communication Interception: Assessing the security implications of intercepting communications between SCADA devices.

Vulnerabilities in SCADA Devices:

Insecure Remote Access: Discussing vulnerabilities introduced by insecure remote access mechanisms to SCADA devices.

Lack of Encryption: Analyzing security risks arising from the absence of robust encryption in SCADA communications.

Inadequate Authentication: Examining challenges associated with weak or inadequate authentication mechanisms in SCADA systems.

Process Automation Systems:

Foundations of Process Automation Systems:

Definition: Unraveling the concept of Process Automation Systems as technologies that automate industrial processes.

Role in Industry: Understanding the significance of process automation in enhancing efficiency and productivity.

Threats to Process Automation Systems:

Data Tampering: Analyzing the risks associated with unauthorized alteration or manipulation of automation system data.

Supply Chain Attacks: Examining the threat posed by compromising components within the supply chain of automation systems.

Human Factor Exploitation: Assessing the security implications of exploiting human vulnerabilities within the automation process.

Vulnerabilities in Process Automation Systems:

Outdated Software: Discussing vulnerabilities introduced by the use of outdated and unpatched software in automation systems.

Insufficient Access Controls: Analyzing security risks arising from inadequate access controls in automation environments.

Lack of Redundancy: Examining challenges associated with the absence of redundancy measures in critical automation components.

By navigating through the intricacies of drones, Industrial Control Systems, SCADA devices, and Process Automation Systems, this chapter equips cybersecurity practitioners with insights into safeguarding against the unique challenges posed by these emerging technologies. Understanding the threats and vulnerabilities is crucial for developing adaptive and resilient cybersecurity strategies in an era of rapid technological advancement.

Practice Questions and Answers

1. Question: What is a common threat associated with access points in wireless communication?

a) Rogue Access Points

b) Biometric Spoofing

c) Data Tampering

d) GPS Spoofing

Answer: a) Rogue Access Points

Explanation: Rogue access points pose a threat by being unauthorized and potentially set up by malicious actors.

2. Question: In virtual private networks (VPNs), what is the primary purpose of encryption protocols?

a) Monitoring network traffic

b) Enhancing device authentication

c) Securing data transmitted over the internet

d) Identifying rogue devices

Answer: c) Securing data transmitted over the internet

Explanation: Encryption protocols in VPNs are designed to secure data transmitted over the internet.

3. Question: What vulnerability is often associated with mobile devices connecting to unsecured Wi-Fi networks?

a) Tailgating

b) GPS Spoofing

c) Man-in-the-Middle Attacks

d) Counterfeit Components

Answer: c) Man-in-the-Middle Attacks

Explanation: Unsecured Wi-Fi networks can expose mobile devices to the risk of man-in-the-middle attacks.

4. Question: In the context of System on a Chip (SoC), what is the potential threat related to side-channel attacks?

a) Unauthorized access to configuration bitstreams

b) Intercepting wireless communication

c) Analyzing unintended information leakage

d) Exploiting hardware backdoors

Answer: c) Analyzing unintended information leakage

Explanation: Side-channel attacks involve exploiting unintended information leakage during chip operations.

5. Question: What is a common threat associated with drones?

a) Data Tampering

b) Insider Threats

c) GPS Spoofing

d) Industrial Control System Exploitation

Answer: c) GPS Spoofing

Explanation: GPS spoofing can manipulate drone navigation systems, leading to unauthorized control.

6. Question: What vulnerability is often found in Supervisory Control and Data Acquisition (SCADA) devices?

a) Lack of Encryption

b) Insider Threats

c) Unauthorized Access

d) Data Tampering

Answer: a) Lack of Encryption

Explanation: SCADA devices may be vulnerable due to the absence of robust encryption in communication.

7. Question: In the realm of Process Automation Systems, what does the term "supply chain attacks" refer to?

a) Unauthorized access to automation systems

b) Manipulation of automation data

c) Compromising components within the supply chain

d) Physical attacks on automation devices

Answer: c) Compromising components within the supply chain

Explanation: Supply chain attacks involve compromising components within the supply chain of automation systems.

8. Question: What is a common threat associated with connected vehicles?

a) Industrial Control System Exploitation

b) Data Interception

c) Tailgating

d) Remote Hacking

Answer: d) Remote Hacking

Explanation: Connected vehicles are susceptible to remote hacking, allowing unauthorized access to vehicle systems.

9. Question: In the context of Industrial Control Systems, what is a potential threat associated with cyber espionage?

a) Data Manipulation

b) Insider Threats

c) GPS Spoofing

d) Nation-state-sponsored spying

Answer: d) Nation-state-sponsored spying

Explanation: Cyber espionage involves spying on ICS for intelligence or strategic purposes.

10. Question: What vulnerability is often associated with Industrial Control Systems using legacy systems?

css

Copy code

a) Insecure Remote Access

b) Lack of Network Segmentation

c) Weak Supply Chain Security

d) Outdated Software

Answer: d) Outdated Software

Explanation: The use of outdated and unsupported legacy systems introduces vulnerabilities in ICS.

11. Question: What threat is associated with unauthorized alteration or manipulation of automation system data?

less

Copy code

a) Insider Threats

b) GPS Spoofing

c) Data Tampering

d) Malware Attacks

Answer: c) Data Tampering

Explanation: Unauthorized alteration or manipulation of data is a threat to process automation systems.

12. Question: In the context of drones, what does the term "data interception" refer to?

a) Unauthorized access to drone control

b) Intercepting data transmitted between drones and ground control stations

c) Physical tampering with drone components

d) Manipulation of GPS signals

Answer: b) Intercepting data transmitted between drones and ground control stations

Explanation: Data interception involves capturing and analyzing data transmitted between drones and ground control.

13. Question: What vulnerability is often associated with SCADA devices using insecure remote access mechanisms?

less

Copy code

a) Lack of Encryption

b) Inadequate Authentication

c) Weak Supply Chain Security

d) Insufficient Access Controls

Answer: b) Inadequate Authentication

Explanation: SCADA devices may be vulnerable due to weak or inadequate authentication mechanisms.

14. Question: What threat is associated with intercepting communications between SCADA devices?

less

Copy code

a) Data Manipulation

b) Communication Interception

c) Insider Threats

d) Physical Attacks

Answer: b) Communication Interception

Explanation: Intercepting communications between SCADA devices can compromise sensitive information.

15. Question: In the context of virtual private networks (VPNs), what does the term "man-in-the-middle attacks" refer to?

kotlin

Copy code

a) Intercepting wireless communication

b) Analyzing unintended information leakage

c) Unauthorized alteration of VPN data

d) Unauthorized individuals gaining control of VPNs

Answer: c) Unauthorized alteration of VPN data

Explanation: Man-in-the-middle attacks involve unauthorized alteration or interception of data in transit.

16. Question: What vulnerability is often found in mobile devices running outdated operating systems?

css

Copy code

a) Lack of Device Encryption

b) Insecure Apps

c) Outdated Software

d) Insufficient Access Controls

Answer: c) Outdated Software

Explanation: Running outdated operating systems introduces security vulnerabilities in mobile devices.

17. Question: What is a common threat associated with access points using default configurations?

less

Copy code

a) Tailgating

b) Rogue Access Points

c) Industrial Control System Exploitation

d) Physical Tampering

Answer: b) Rogue Access Points

Explanation: Default configurations in access points may lead to the creation of rogue access points by malicious actors.

18. Question: In the context of drones, what is the potential threat related to physical tampering?

css

Copy code

a) Unauthorized access to drone control

b) Manipulation of GPS signals

c) Physical attacks on drones

d) Tampering or hijacking of drones

Answer: d) Tampering or hijacking of drones

Explanation: Physical tampering poses a threat to the integrity and control of drones.

19. Question: What vulnerability is often associated with process automation systems lacking access controls?

css

Copy code

a) Lack of Network Segmentation

b) Weak Supply Chain Security

c) Insufficient Access Controls

d) Lack of Redundancy

Answer: c) Insufficient Access Controls

Explanation: Inadequate access controls introduce vulnerabilities in process automation systems.

20. Question: In the context of System on a Chip (SoC), what does the term "counterfeit components" refer to?

css

Copy code

a) Unauthorized alteration of SoC configuration

b) Intercepting SoC communications

c) Power Analysis Attacks on SoC

d) Infiltration of fake or altered SoC components

Answer: d) Infiltration of fake or altered SoC components

Explanation: Counterfeit components in SoC involve the use of fake or altered components.

21. Question: What threat is associated with manipulating GPS signals to deceive drone navigation systems?

css

Copy code

a) Data Interception

b) GPS Spoofing

c) Unauthorized access to drone control

d) Physical attacks on drones

Answer: b) GPS Spoofing

Explanation: GPS spoofing involves manipulating GPS signals to deceive navigation systems.

22. Question: In the context of virtual private networks (VPNs), what is the potential threat related to protocol vulnerabilities?

css

Copy code

a) Man-in-the-Middle Attacks

b) Unauthorized access to VPNs

c) Data Interception

d) Denial-of-Service (DoS) Attacks

Answer: a) Man-in-the-Middle Attacks

Explanation: Protocol vulnerabilities in VPNs can be exploited for man-in-the-middle attacks.

23. Question: What vulnerability is often associated with mobile devices lacking proper encryption measures?

less

Copy code

a) Lack of Device Encryption

b) Insufficient Access Controls

c) Outdated Software

d) Weak Authentication

Answer: a) Lack of Device Encryption

Explanation: Mobile devices without proper encryption measures are vulnerable to unauthorized access.

24. Question: What is a common threat associated with connected vehicles?

less

Copy code

a) Industrial Control System Exploitation

b) Remote Hacking

c) Data Interception

d) Unauthorized alteration of vehicle data

Answer: b) Remote Hacking

Explanation: Connected vehicles are susceptible to remote hacking for unauthorized access.

25. Question: What vulnerability is often found in drones using default configurations?

css

Copy code

a) Physical Tampering

b) Lack of Encryption

c) Insufficient Access Controls

d) Rogue Access Points

Answer: d) Rogue Access Points

Explanation: Default configurations in drones may lead to the creation of rogue access points.

26. Question: In the context of Industrial Control Systems, what does the term "insider threats" refer to?

kotlin

Copy code

a) Unauthorized alteration of ICS data

b) Nation-state-sponsored spying

c) Unauthorized access by malicious insiders

d) Exploitation of ICS components within the supply chain

Answer: c) Unauthorized access by malicious insiders

Explanation: Insider threats involve authorized personnel exploiting their access to compromise ICS.

27. Question: What threat is associated with intercepting data transmitted between drones and ground control stations?

css

Copy code

a) Unauthorized access to drone control

b) Industrial Control System Exploitation

c) Data Interception

d) Unauthorized alteration of drone data

Answer: c) Data Interception

Explanation: Intercepting data between drones and ground control stations can compromise sensitive information.

28. Question: In the context of drones, what is the potential threat related to GPS spoofing?

vbnet

Copy code

a) Physical attacks on drones

b) Unauthorized access to drone control

c) Manipulation of GPS signals

d) Data Interception

Answer: b) Unauthorized access to drone control

Explanation: GPS spoofing can lead to unauthorized access and control of drones.

29. Question: What vulnerability is often associated with SCADA devices lacking proper access controls?

css

Copy code

a) Lack of Encryption

b) Weak Supply Chain Security

c) Insufficient Access Controls

d) Inadequate Authentication

Answer: c) Insufficient Access Controls

Explanation: SCADA devices without proper access controls may be vulnerable to unauthorized access.

30. Question: In the context of Process Automation Systems, what does the term "human factor exploitation" refer to?

a) Unauthorized access to automation systems

b) Manipulation of automation data

c) Exploiting human vulnerabilities within the automation process

d) Compromising components within the supply chain

Answer: c) Exploiting human vulnerabilities within the automation process

Explanation: Human factor exploitation involves exploiting vulnerabilities in human interactions within the automation process.

Chapter 6: Threats Vulnerabilities Associated with Operatinhg in the Cloud

In the dynamic landscape of cloud computing, this chapter unravels the intricate web of threats and vulnerabilities inherent in leveraging cloud services. From the diversity of cloud service models and deployment options to the innovative realm of serverless architecture, organizations face a myriad of challenges in securing their digital assets within the expansive domain of the cloud.

Cloud Service Models:

Infrastructure as a Service (IaaS):

Definition: Unveiling the core concept of IaaS, where virtualized computing resources are provided over the internet.

Threats: Analyzing potential threats such as unauthorized access to virtual machines and data breaches within IaaS environments.

Vulnerabilities: Examining vulnerabilities introduced by misconfigurations, inadequate access controls, and insecure APIs in IaaS offerings.

Platform as a Service (PaaS):

Overview: Understanding PaaS as a cloud service model that provides a platform allowing customers to develop, run, and manage applications.

Threat Landscape: Analyzing threats related to data exposure, insecure application development practices, and service provider breaches in PaaS environments.

Vulnerability Analysis: Examining vulnerabilities arising from weak application security, insufficient data encryption, and inadequate identity management within PaaS solutions.

Software as a Service (SaaS):

Introduction: Unraveling SaaS as a cloud model delivering software applications over the internet.

Threats to SaaS: Analyzing threats such as unauthorized access, data loss, and service provider outages within the SaaS paradigm.

Vulnerabilities in SaaS: Examining vulnerabilities introduced by weak authentication, insecure data storage practices, and reliance on third-party security measures in SaaS offerings.

Cloud Deployment Models:

Public Cloud:

Definition: Understanding the concept of public cloud, where cloud services are offered by third-party providers on a shared infrastructure.

Threats in Public Cloud: Analyzing threats related to shared resources, multi-tenancy issues, and potential exposure to untrusted networks in public cloud environments.

Vulnerabilities: Examining vulnerabilities introduced by insecure interfaces, inadequate network segmentation, and lack of control over underlying infrastructure in public cloud deployments.

Private Cloud:

Overview: Unveiling private cloud as a cloud infrastructure solely dedicated to a single organization, offering enhanced control and security.

Threat Landscape in Private Cloud: Analyzing threats associated with insider attacks, misconfigured security controls, and potential lack of scalability in private cloud environments.

Vulnerability Analysis: Examining vulnerabilities introduced by inadequate access controls, misconfigured virtualization platforms, and potential neglect of security updates in private cloud deployments.

Hybrid Cloud:

Definition: Understanding hybrid cloud as a combination of public and private cloud infrastructures, providing flexibility and data portability.

Threats to Hybrid Cloud: Analyzing threats related to data integration challenges, interoperability issues, and potential security gaps in hybrid cloud environments.

Vulnerabilities in Hybrid Cloud: Examining vulnerabilities introduced by inadequate data encryption during transit, insecure APIs, and potential inconsistencies in security policies across public and private components of hybrid cloud deployments.

Serverless Architecture:

Introduction to Serverless Architecture:

Definition: Unraveling serverless architecture as a cloud computing model where applications are developed and run without managing underlying infrastructure.

Threat Landscape in Serverless: Analyzing threats such as insecure deployment configurations, inadequate authentication mechanisms, and potential abuse of event-driven architectures in serverless environments.

Vulnerability Analysis: Examining vulnerabilities introduced by insufficient isolation of functions, lack of proper logging and monitoring, and potential risks associated with third-party dependencies in serverless applications.

Benefits and Challenges:

Advantages: Understanding the benefits of serverless architecture, including scalability, cost efficiency, and reduced operational overhead.

Challenges: Analyzing challenges such as security concerns, limited control over underlying infrastructure, and potential performance issues in serverless computing environments.

By navigating through the nuances of cloud service models, deployment options, and the transformative landscape of serverless architecture, this chapter equips cybersecurity practitioners with insights to address the unique challenges posed by operating in the cloud. Understanding the threats and vulnerabilities is essential for developing robust security strategies in an era where cloud technologies play a pivotal role in digital transformation.

In the ever-evolving landscape of cloud computing, this chapter explores advanced security practices crucial for safeguarding digital assets in the cloud. Delving into the intricacies of Infrastructure as Code (IaC), Insecure Application Programming Interfaces (APIs), Improper Key Management, Unprotected Storage, and Logging and Monitoring, organizations can fortify their cloud defenses against an array of sophisticated threats.

Infrastructure as Code (IaC):

Foundations of IaC:

Definition: Unveiling Infrastructure as Code as a methodology for managing and provisioning infrastructure through machine-readable scripts.

Security Benefits: Analyzing the security advantages of IaC, including consistency, version control, and automated compliance.

Threats in IaC Environments:

Misconfigurations: Analyzing the threat posed by misconfigurations in IaC scripts leading to insecure cloud infrastructures.

Unauthorized Changes: Examining the risk of unauthorized modifications to IaC code, compromising the integrity of cloud deployments.

Security Best Practices:

Automated Scanning: Understanding the importance of automated scanning tools to identify vulnerabilities in IaC scripts.

Continuous Monitoring: Emphasizing the need for continuous monitoring to detect and remediate security issues in real-time.

Insecure Application Programming Interfaces (APIs):

APIs in Cloud Computing:

Role of APIs: Understanding the integral role of APIs in enabling communication between cloud services and applications.

Security Implications: Analyzing the security implications of insecure API design, implementation, and usage.

Common API Threats:

Injection Attacks: Examining the threat of injection attacks, where malicious code is injected into API requests.

Inadequate Authentication: Analyzing the risk of unauthorized access due to weak or insufficient authentication mechanisms in APIs.

Mitigating API Risks:

Secure Authentication: Emphasizing the implementation of robust authentication mechanisms, such as OAuth or API keys.

API Rate Limiting: Utilizing rate-limiting measures to prevent abuse and protect against denial-of-service (DoS) attacks on APIs.

Improper Key Management:

Key Management Fundamentals:

Key Generation: Understanding the key generation process and the importance of entropy in creating strong cryptographic keys.

Key Storage: Analyzing secure key storage practices to prevent unauthorized access to cryptographic keys.

Key-related Threats:

Key Exposure: Examining the threat of key exposure, where cryptographic keys are unintentionally disclosed or compromised.

Insufficient Rotation: Analyzing the risk associated with not regularly rotating cryptographic keys, increasing vulnerability to attacks.

Key Management Best Practices:

Automated Rotation: Implementing automated key rotation processes to ensure the timely and secure rotation of cryptographic keys.

Secure Storage Vaults: Leveraging secure key storage vaults and Hardware Security Modules (HSMs) for enhanced protection.

Unprotected Storage:

Storage Security Overview:

Types of Cloud Storage: Understanding various types of cloud storage, including object storage, block storage, and file storage.

Security Implications: Analyzing security implications related to misconfigured storage settings, unencrypted data, and unauthorized access.

Storage-related Threats:

Data Exposure: Examining the threat of unauthorized access or exposure of sensitive data stored in the cloud.

Data Retention Risks: Analyzing risks associated with improper data retention policies, leading to unintended data exposure.

Securing Cloud Storage:

Encryption at Rest and in Transit: Implementing robust encryption mechanisms to protect data both at rest and during transit.

Access Controls: Utilizing fine-grained access controls to restrict and monitor access to stored data based on roles and permissions.

Logging and Monitoring:

Importance of Logging and Monitoring:

Visibility and Detection: Understanding the crucial role of logging and monitoring in providing visibility into cloud environments and detecting suspicious activities.

Incident Response: Analyzing the contribution of effective logging to incident response and forensic investigations.

Logging Best Practices:

Comprehensive Logging: Implementing comprehensive logging of relevant events, including authentication attempts, resource provisioning, and security policy violations.

Log Retention Policies: Defining log retention policies to ensure the availability of historical data for compliance and investigation purposes.

Continuous Monitoring:

Real-time Alerts: Establishing real-time alerting mechanisms based on predefined security thresholds to enable timely response to security incidents.

Behavioral Analytics: Utilizing behavioral analytics to detect anomalous patterns and potential security breaches through continuous monitoring.

By delving into the nuances of Infrastructure as Code, Insecure APIs, Improper Key Management, Unprotected Storage, and Logging and Monitoring, this chapter equips cybersecurity professionals with advanced strategies to fortify cloud security measures. The insights provided empower organizations to navigate the complexities of cloud computing securely, ensuring the protection of sensitive data and the resilience of cloud-based infrastructures against emerging threats.

Practice Questions and Answers

1. Question: What is a common threat associated with misconfigurations in Infrastructure as Code (IaC) scripts?

a) Data Breaches

b) Unauthorized Code Modifications

c) Distributed Denial of Service (DDoS) Attacks

d) Insider Threats

Answer: b) Unauthorized Code Modifications

Explanation: Misconfigurations in IaC scripts can lead to unauthorized modifications, compromising the integrity of cloud deployments.

2. Question: In the context of Insecure Application Programming Interfaces (APIs), what is the primary risk of inadequate authentication mechanisms?

a) Injection Attacks

b) Unauthorized Access

c) Data Exposure

d) Distributed Denial of Service (DDoS) Attacks

Answer: b) Unauthorized Access

Explanation: Inadequate authentication mechanisms in APIs can lead to unauthorized access, posing a security risk.

3. Question: What is a potential threat associated with improper key management in cloud environments?

a) Data Retention Risks

b) Key Exposure

c) Injection Attacks

d) Unauthorized Code Modifications

Answer: b) Key Exposure

Explanation: Improper key management can lead to the exposure of cryptographic keys, compromising security.

4. Question: In the realm of Unprotected Storage, what risk is associated with misconfigured storage settings?

a) Injection Attacks

b) Unauthorized Access

c) Data Exposure

d) Data Retention Risks

Answer: c) Data Exposure

Explanation: Misconfigured storage settings can lead to unauthorized access and exposure of sensitive data.

5. Question: What is the primary purpose of logging in cloud environments?

a) Real-time Alerts

b) Data Encryption

c) Behavioral Analytics

d) Unauthorized Code Modifications

Answer: a) Real-time Alerts

Explanation: Logging in cloud environments provides real-time alerts, aiding in timely incident response.

6. Question: What threat is associated with unauthorized access to Infrastructure as Code (IaC) scripts?

a) Data Breaches

b) Insider Threats

c) Injection Attacks

d) Unauthorized Code Modifications

Answer: d) Unauthorized Code Modifications

Explanation: Unauthorized access to IaC scripts can lead to unauthorized code modifications and compromise cloud deployments.

7. Question: In the context of Insecure Application Programming Interfaces (APIs), what is an example of an injection attack?

a) Cross-Site Scripting (XSS)

b) SQL Injection

c) Man-in-the-Middle Attacks

d) Denial-of-Service (DoS) Attacks

Answer: b) SQL Injection

Explanation: SQL injection is an example of an injection attack in APIs where malicious code is injected into API requests.

8. Question: What is a common vulnerability associated with inadequate authentication mechanisms in APIs?

a) Insufficient Logging

b) Weak Data Encryption

c) Lack of Rate Limiting

d) Insecure Access Controls

Answer: d) Insecure Access Controls

Explanation: Inadequate authentication can lead to insecure access controls, allowing unauthorized users to access API resources.

9. Question: What is a potential risk of inadequate key rotation in key management?

a) Data Exposure

b) Unauthorized Code Modifications

c) Injection Attacks

d) Key Exposure

Answer: d) Key Exposure

Explanation: Inadequate key rotation increases the risk of key exposure, compromising cryptographic keys.

10. Question: In the context of Unprotected Storage, what vulnerability is introduced by unauthorized access to cloud storage?

less

Copy code

a) Lack of Data Encryption

b) Data Retention Risks

c) Inadequate Access Controls

d) Misconfigured Storage Settings

Answer: c) Inadequate Access Controls

Explanation: Unauthorized access introduces inadequate access controls, posing a security vulnerability.

11. Question: What is the primary purpose of continuous monitoring in cloud environments?

a) Data Encryption

b) Real-time Incident Response

c) Behavioral Analytics

d) Unauthorized Code Modifications

Answer: b) Real-time Incident Response

Explanation: Continuous monitoring facilitates real-time incident response by providing visibility into cloud environments.

12. Question: In the realm of Infrastructure as Code (IaC), what is a potential risk of misconfigurations?

css

Copy code

a) Unauthorized Code Modifications

b) Insider Threats

c) Data Breaches

d) Distributed Denial of Service (DDoS) Attacks

Answer: c) Data Breaches

Explanation: Misconfigurations in IaC scripts can lead to data breaches, compromising sensitive information.

13. Question: In the context of Insecure Application Programming Interfaces (APIs), what risk is associated with insufficient rate limiting?

css

Copy code

a) Unauthorized Access

b) Injection Attacks

c) Denial-of-Service (DoS) Attacks

d) Data Exposure

Answer: c) Denial-of-Service (DoS) Attacks

Explanation: Insufficient rate limiting can lead to Denial-of-Service (DoS) attacks, disrupting API services.

14. Question: What vulnerability is often associated with improper key storage practices?

less

Copy code

a) Lack of Data Encryption

b) Insufficient Logging

c) Data Retention Risks

d) Unauthorized Code Modifications

Answer: a) Lack of Data Encryption

Explanation: Improper key storage practices can lead to the lack of data encryption, exposing sensitive information.

15. Question: In the context of Unprotected Storage, what is a risk associated with misconfigured storage settings?

less

Copy code

a) Unauthorized Access

b) Data Retention Risks

c) Injection Attacks

d) Insider Threats

Answer: b) Data Retention Risks

Explanation: Misconfigured storage settings can lead to data retention risks, impacting data security and compliance.

16. Question: What is the primary purpose of logging in cloud environments?

a) Real-time Alerts

b) Data Encryption

c) Behavioral Analytics

d) Unauthorized Code Modifications

Answer: a) Real-time Alerts

Explanation: Logging provides real-time alerts, aiding in the timely detection and response to security incidents.

17. Question: In the context of Infrastructure as Code (IaC), what is a common threat associated with unauthorized code modifications?

less

Copy code

a) Insider Threats

b) Misconfigurations

c) Distributed Denial of Service (DDoS) Attacks

d) Data Breaches

Answer: b) Misconfigurations

Explanation: Unauthorized code modifications can lead to misconfigurations, impacting the integrity of cloud deployments.

18. Question: What is a potential threat associated with weak data encryption in Unprotected Storage?

less

Copy code

a) Data Exposure

b) Unauthorized Access

c) Injection Attacks

d) Insider Threats

Answer: a) Data Exposure

Explanation: Weak data encryption can lead to data exposure, compromising the confidentiality of stored information.

19. Question: In the context of Logging and Monitoring, what is the significance of behavioral analytics?

css

Copy code

a) Real-time Incident Response

b) Data Encryption

c) Detection of Anomalous Patterns

d) Unauthorized Code Modifications

Answer: c) Detection of Anomalous Patterns

Explanation: Behavioral analytics helps in detecting anomalous patterns and potential security breaches through continuous monitoring.

20. Question: What vulnerability is often associated with inadequate access controls in cloud storage?

less

Copy code

a) Lack of Data Encryption

b) Unauthorized Access

c) Data Retention Risks

d) Misconfigured Storage Settings

Answer: b) Unauthorized Access

Explanation: Inadequate access controls can lead to unauthorized access to cloud storage, compromising data security.

21. Question: In the realm of Infrastructure as Code (IaC), what is a common vulnerability associated with insider threats?

css

Copy code

a) Unauthorized Code Modifications

b) Data Breaches

c) Misconfigurations

d) Distributed Denial of Service (DDoS) Attacks

Answer: c) Misconfigurations

Explanation: Insider threats can lead to misconfigurations, impacting the integrity of IaC scripts and cloud deployments.

22. Question: What is the primary risk associated with injection attacks in Insecure Application Programming Interfaces (APIs)?

less

Copy code

a) Data Exposure

b) Unauthorized Access

c) Denial-of-Service (DoS) Attacks

d) Unauthorized Code Modifications

Answer: a) Data Exposure

Explanation: Injection attacks can lead to data exposure, compromising the confidentiality of API data.

23. Question: In the context of Improper Key Management, what risk is associated with insufficient rotation of cryptographic keys?

less

Copy code

a) Key Exposure

b) Unauthorized Code Modifications

c) Injection Attacks

d) Data Retention Risks

Answer: a) Key Exposure

Explanation: Insufficient key rotation increases the risk of key exposure, compromising cryptographic keys.

24. Question: What vulnerability is often associated with inadequate access controls in Unprotected Storage?

less

Copy code

a) Lack of Data Encryption

b) Unauthorized Access

c) Data Retention Risks

d) Misconfigured Storage Settings

Answer: b) Unauthorized Access

Explanation: Inadequate access controls can lead to unauthorized access to storage, compromising data security.

25. Question: In the context of Logging and Monitoring, what is the purpose of comprehensive logging?

css

Copy code

a) Behavioral Analytics

b) Real-time Alerts

c) Log Retention Policies

d) Detection of Anomalous Patterns

Answer: c) Log Retention Policies

Explanation: Comprehensive logging supports log retention policies, ensuring availability of historical data for compliance and investigation.

26. Question: What is a common threat associated with inadequate key rotation in key management?

css

Copy code

a) Key Exposure

b) Unauthorized Code Modifications

c) Injection Attacks

d) Data Retention Risks

Answer: d) Data Retention Risks

Explanation: Inadequate key rotation increases the risk of data retention risks, impacting security.

27. Question: In the context of Unprotected Storage, what vulnerability is introduced by misconfigured storage settings?

less

Copy code

a) Data Exposure

b) Unauthorized Access

c) Data Retention Risks

d) Insider Threats

Answer: a) Data Exposure

Explanation: Misconfigured storage settings can lead to data exposure, compromising data confidentiality.

28. Question: What is a potential threat associated with misconfigurations in Logging and Monitoring?

less

Copy code

a) Insider Threats

b) Unauthorized Code Modifications

c) Lack of Behavioral Analytics

d) Detection of Anomalous Patterns

Answer: a) Insider Threats

Explanation: Misconfigurations in logging and monitoring can lead to insider threats, compromising the effectiveness of security measures.

29. Question: In the realm of Insecure Application Programming Interfaces (APIs), what is a common risk associated with injection attacks?

css

Copy code

a) Data Exposure

b) Unauthorized Access

c) Denial-of-Service (DoS) Attacks

d) Unauthorized Code Modifications

Answer: c) Denial-of-Service (DoS) Attacks

Explanation: Injection attacks can lead to Denial-of-Service (DoS) attacks, disrupting API services.

30. Question: What vulnerability is often associated with weak data encryption in Logging and Monitoring?

less

Copy code

a) Lack of Data Encryption

b) Unauthorized Access

c) Data Retention Risks

d) Misconfigured Storage Settings

Answer: a) Lack of Data Encryption

Explanation: Weak data encryption in logging and monitoring can compromise the confidentiality of log data.

Chapter 7: Mitigating Attacks and Software Vulnerabilities

In the complex landscape of cybersecurity, mitigating attacks and addressing software vulnerabilities are paramount to ensuring the resilience of systems and the protection of sensitive information. This chapter navigates through various attack types, vulnerabilities, and strategies for safeguarding software and systems. Part 2 specifically focuses on Software and Systems Security, providing insights into fortifying digital assets against evolving threats.

Attack Types:

Social Engineering Attacks:

Overview: Understanding the manipulation of individuals to disclose confidential information or perform actions detrimental to security.

Mitigation Strategies: Analyzing the importance of user awareness training, multi-factor authentication, and robust access controls to counter social engineering attacks.

Malware Attacks:

Introduction: Unraveling the diverse forms of malicious software designed to compromise systems and steal sensitive data.

Mitigation Measures: Exploring the use of antivirus software, endpoint protection, and regular system scans to mitigate the risks posed by malware attacks.

Denial-of-Service (DoS) Attacks:

Definition: Understanding attacks that disrupt the availability of services by overwhelming systems with excessive traffic.

Mitigation Techniques: Analyzing the deployment of DoS mitigation tools, traffic filtering, and the use of Content Delivery Networks (CDNs) to protect against DoS attacks.

Vulnerabilities:

Software Vulnerabilities:

Overview: Identifying weaknesses in software that can be exploited by attackers to compromise system integrity.

Mitigation Approaches: Exploring the importance of regular software updates, patch management, and secure coding practices to address and mitigate software vulnerabilities.

Network Vulnerabilities:

Definition: Understanding weaknesses in network infrastructure that can be exploited to gain unauthorized access or disrupt communication.

Mitigation Strategies: Analyzing the use of firewalls, intrusion detection/prevention systems, and regular network security assessments to address and mitigate network vulnerabilities.

Human-Related Vulnerabilities:

Overview: Recognizing vulnerabilities introduced by human actions, such as negligence, unintentional errors, or malicious insider activities.

Mitigation Measures: Exploring the role of user training, access controls, and employee awareness programs to mitigate vulnerabilities associated with human actions.

Part 2: Software and Systems Security:

Secure Software Development Practices:

Foundations: Understanding the significance of integrating security measures into the software development lifecycle.

Mitigation Techniques: Analyzing secure coding practices, code reviews, and automated testing tools to enhance the security of software applications.

Systems Hardening:

Definition: Implementing measures to reduce the attack surface and strengthen the security posture of systems.

Mitigation Approaches: Exploring the use of system configuration reviews, least privilege principles, and regular system audits to harden and secure systems.

Incident Response and Recovery:

Incident Handling: Understanding the process of identifying, responding to, and mitigating security incidents.

Mitigation Strategies: Analyzing the importance of incident response planning, continuous monitoring, and post-incident reviews to enhance the resilience of systems.

Practice Questions and Answers

Attack Types:

Question: What is the primary goal of a social engineering attack?

a) Gain unauthorized access to networks

b) Overwhelm systems with traffic

c) Exploit software vulnerabilities

d) Manipulate individuals for information or actions

Answer: d) Manipulate individuals for information or actions

Explanation: Social engineering attacks aim to manipulate individuals into divulging confidential information or performing actions that could compromise security.

Question: How can organizations mitigate the risks associated with social engineering attacks?

a) Implementing multi-factor authentication

b) Conducting regular system scans

c) Deploying intrusion detection systems

d) Providing user awareness training

Answer: d) Providing user awareness training

Explanation: User awareness training is crucial to mitigating social engineering risks by educating individuals about potential threats.

Question: What is the purpose of antivirus software in mitigating malware attacks?

a) Blocking malicious websites

b) Encrypting sensitive data

c) Detecting and removing malicious software

d) Filtering network traffic

Answer: c) Detecting and removing malicious software

Explanation: Antivirus software is designed to detect and remove malicious software, providing protection against malware attacks.

Question: How can organizations defend against Denial-of-Service (DoS) attacks?

a) Implementing firewalls and intrusion detection systems

b) Using Content Delivery Networks (CDNs)

c) Encrypting data in transit

d) Conducting regular penetration testing

Answer: b) Using Content Delivery Networks (CDNs)

Explanation: CDNs help mitigate DoS attacks by distributing traffic and providing additional layers of protection.

Vulnerabilities:

Question: What is the purpose of regular software updates in addressing software vulnerabilities?

a) Enhancing system performance

b) Introducing new features

c) Fixing security weaknesses

d) Improving user interface design

Answer: c) Fixing security weaknesses

Explanation: Regular software updates often include patches that address security vulnerabilities and enhance the overall security of the software.

Question: How can organizations mitigate network vulnerabilities?

a) Implementing secure coding practices

b) Conducting regular network security assessments

c) Encrypting sensitive data

d) Providing employee awareness training

Answer: b) Conducting regular network security assessments

Explanation: Regular network security assessments help identify and address vulnerabilities in the network infrastructure.

Question: What is a common mitigation measure for human-related vulnerabilities?

a) Using intrusion detection systems

b) Conducting penetration testing

c) Implementing access controls

d) Providing user training and awareness programs

Answer: d) Providing user training and awareness programs

Explanation: User training and awareness programs are essential in mitigating vulnerabilities associated with human actions.

Part 2: Software and Systems Security:

Question: What is the primary focus of secure software development practices?

a) Maximizing software features

b) Minimizing development costs

c) Integrating security into the development lifecycle

d) Accelerating development timelines

Answer: c) Integrating security into the development lifecycle

Explanation: Secure software development practices focus on integrating security measures throughout the entire software development lifecycle.

Question: What does systems hardening aim to achieve?

a) Maximizing system performance

b) Minimizing system complexity

c) Reducing the attack surface and strengthening security

d) Accelerating system deployment

Answer: c) Reducing the attack surface and strengthening security

Explanation: Systems hardening aims to reduce vulnerabilities by minimizing the attack surface and strengthening the overall security of systems.

Question: What is the purpose of incident response planning?

a) Preventing all security incidents

b) Identifying, responding to, and mitigating security incidents

c) Recovering from incidents without investigation

d) Ignoring security incidents to avoid detection

Answer: b) Identifying, responding to, and mitigating security incidents

Explanation: Incident response planning focuses on effectively identifying, responding to, and mitigating security incidents to minimize their impact.

Question: How can organizations enhance incident response capabilities?

a) Ignoring incident reports

b) Conducting post-incident reviews

c) Disabling real-time monitoring

d) Avoiding incident detection tools

Answer: b) Conducting post-incident reviews

Explanation: Post-incident reviews help organizations learn from security incidents and improve incident response capabilities.

Question: What is the primary goal of systems hardening?

a) Maximizing system complexity

b) Minimizing system performance

c) Reducing the attack surface and strengthening security

d) Accelerating system vulnerabilities

Answer: c) Reducing the attack surface and strengthening security

Explanation: Systems hardening aims to reduce vulnerabilities by minimizing the attack surface and strengthening system security.

Question: How does secure software development contribute to overall cybersecurity?

a) By ignoring security concerns

b) By accelerating development timelines

c) By integrating security measures into the development lifecycle

d) By avoiding security testing

Answer: c) By integrating security measures into the development lifecycle

Explanation: Secure software development involves integrating security measures throughout the development lifecycle to enhance overall cybersecurity.

Question: What role does user awareness training play in mitigating social engineering attacks?

a) It increases attack surface

b) It introduces vulnerabilities

c) It mitigates risks by educating users

d) It encourages sharing sensitive information

Answer: c) It mitigates risks by educating users

Explanation: User awareness training helps mitigate social engineering risks by educating users about potential threats and how to avoid them.

Question: Why is it important to conduct regular network security assessments?

a) To introduce vulnerabilities

b) To maximize system performance

c) To identify and address vulnerabilities in the network infrastructure

d) To minimize system complexity

Answer: c) To identify and address vulnerabilities in the network infrastructure

Explanation: Regular network security assessments help identify and address vulnerabilities in the network infrastructure.

Question: What is the purpose of providing employee awareness training to mitigate human-related vulnerabilities?

a) To increase the complexity of systems

b) To introduce security risks

c) To mitigate vulnerabilities associated with human actions

d) To encourage unsafe behaviors

Answer: c) To mitigate vulnerabilities associated with human actions

Explanation: Employee awareness training helps mitigate vulnerabilities associated with human actions by educating employees about security best practices.

Question: What is the significance of incident response planning in cybersecurity?

a) To avoid detection of security incidents

b) To recover from incidents without investigation

c) To identify, respond to, and mitigate security incidents effectively

d) To increase the impact of security incidents

Answer: c) To identify, respond to, and mitigate security incidents effectively

Explanation: Incident response planning is significant in cybersecurity to effectively identify, respond to, and mitigate security incidents.

Question: How does regular software updating contribute to addressing vulnerabilities?

a) By introducing new security weaknesses

b) By minimizing system performance

c) By fixing security weaknesses and enhancing overall security

d) By accelerating the development timeline

Answer: c) By fixing security weaknesses and enhancing overall security

Explanation: Regular software updates include patches that fix security weaknesses and enhance the overall security of the software.

Question: In the context of Denial-of-Service (DoS) attacks, how does using Content Delivery Networks (CDNs) help?

a) By introducing excessive traffic

b) By disrupting system availability

c) By overwhelming systems with traffic

d) By distributing traffic and providing additional protection

Answer: d) By distributing traffic and providing additional protection

Explanation: CDNs help mitigate DoS attacks by distributing traffic and providing additional layers of protection.

Question: What role does incident response play in minimizing the impact of security incidents?

a) To maximize the impact of security incidents

b) To avoid detection of security incidents

c) To identify, respond to, and mitigate security incidents effectively

d) To encourage the occurrence of security incidents

Answer: c) To identify, respond to, and mitigate security incidents effectively

Explanation: Incident response aims to identify, respond to, and mitigate security incidents effectively to minimize their impact.

Question: How does systems hardening contribute to reducing vulnerabilities?

a) By maximizing system complexity

b) By minimizing system performance

c) By reducing the attack surface and strengthening security

d) By accelerating system vulnerabilities

Answer: c) By reducing the attack surface and strengthening security

Explanation: Systems hardening contributes to reducing vulnerabilities by minimizing the attack surface and strengthening system security.

Question: What is the primary purpose of conducting post-incident reviews?

a) To maximize the impact of security incidents

b) To avoid detection of security incidents

c) To recover from incidents without investigation

d) To learn from incidents and improve incident response capabilities

Answer: d) To learn from incidents and improve incident response capabilities

Explanation: Post-incident reviews help organizations learn from incidents and improve incident response capabilities.

Question: What mitigation measure is crucial for addressing malware attacks?

a) Regular system scans

b) Avoiding user awareness training

c) Disabling antivirus software

d) Ignoring security patches

Answer: a) Regular system scans

Explanation: Regular system scans are crucial for detecting and removing malware, contributing to the mitigation of malware attacks.

Question: How does providing user awareness training contribute to mitigating social engineering attacks?

a) By encouraging sharing of sensitive information

b) By minimizing user awareness

c) By introducing vulnerabilities

d) By educating users about potential threats

Answer: d) By educating users about potential threats

Explanation: User awareness training helps mitigate social engineering attacks by educating users about potential threats and how to avoid them.

Question: What is the role of network security assessments in addressing vulnerabilities?

a) To introduce vulnerabilities in the network

b) To minimize system performance

c) To identify and address vulnerabilities in the network infrastructure

d) To avoid detection of network vulnerabilities

Answer: c) To identify and address vulnerabilities in the network infrastructure

Explanation: Network security assessments help identify and address vulnerabilities in the network infrastructure.

Question: How does conducting regular penetration testing contribute to network security?

a) By minimizing system complexity

b) By avoiding detection of vulnerabilities

c) By introducing vulnerabilities in the network

d) By identifying and addressing vulnerabilities

Answer: d) By identifying and addressing vulnerabilities

Explanation: Regular penetration testing helps identify and address vulnerabilities, contributing to enhanced network security.

Question: What is the purpose of conducting post-incident reviews in incident response?

a) To avoid detection of incidents

b) To maximize the impact of incidents

c) To recover from incidents without investigation

d) To learn from incidents and improve incident response capabilities

Answer: d) To learn from incidents and improve incident response capabilities

Explanation: Post-incident reviews help organizations learn from incidents and improve incident response capabilities.

Question: How can organizations address human-related vulnerabilities?

a) By minimizing user awareness training

b) By encouraging unsafe behaviors

c) By implementing access controls

d) By avoiding employee awareness programs

Answer: c) By implementing access controls

Explanation: Implementing access controls is one way to address human-related vulnerabilities by restricting unauthorized access.

Question: What is the role of regular software updates in addressing vulnerabilities?

a) To introduce new security weaknesses

b) To minimize system performance

c) To fix security weaknesses and enhance overall security

d) To accelerate the development timeline

Answer: c) To fix security weaknesses and enhance overall security

Explanation: Regular software updates include patches that fix security weaknesses and enhance the overall security of the software.

Question: How can organizations enhance incident response capabilities?

a) By avoiding incident detection tools

b) By ignoring incident reports

c) By conducting post-incident reviews

d) By maximizing the impact of incidents

Answer: c) By conducting post-incident reviews

Explanation: Conducting post-incident reviews helps organizations learn from incidents and improve incident response capabilities.

Chapter 8: Security Solutions for Infrastructure Management

In the dynamic landscape of cybersecurity, the effective management of infrastructure is fundamental to ensuring the confidentiality, integrity, and availability of digital assets. This chapter explores key security solutions for infrastructure management, comparing the strengths and considerations of cloud versus on-premises solutions. Additionally, it delves into critical aspects of network architecture, visualization, containerization, and network segmentation, providing insights into fortifying infrastructure against evolving threats.

Cloud vs. On-Premises Solutions:

Comparative Analysis:

Overview: Evaluating the advantages and challenges of cloud and on-premises solutions in the context of security and infrastructure management.

Considerations: Exploring factors such as scalability, cost, control, and compliance to guide decision-making in choosing between cloud and on-premises models.

Hybrid Approaches:

Definition: Understanding the hybrid model, which combines elements of both cloud and on-premises solutions to achieve a balanced and flexible infrastructure.

Security Implications: Analyzing the security considerations and best practices for implementing and securing hybrid infrastructure.

Network Architecture:

Secure Network Design:

Foundations: Establishing the principles of secure network design to create a resilient and well-protected infrastructure.

Risk Mitigation: Examining techniques such as network segmentation, encryption, and intrusion detection to mitigate risks and enhance network security.

Visualization:

Visualizing Infrastructure:

Importance: Recognizing the significance of visualizing infrastructure components and relationships for effective monitoring and response.

Tools and Techniques: Exploring visualization tools and techniques that aid in comprehending complex infrastructures and identifying anomalies.

Containerization:

Container Security:

Container Technology: Understanding the principles of containerization and its impact on the agility and efficiency of infrastructure deployment.

Security Measures: Examining container security practices, including image integrity, isolation, and orchestration tools, to ensure the secure utilization of containers.

Network Segmentation:

Segmentation Strategies:

Definition: Defining network segmentation as a strategy to divide networks into isolated segments for enhanced security.

Implementation: Exploring the implementation of network segmentation through techniques such as VLANs, firewalls, and micro-segmentation to protect critical assets.

In the ever-evolving landscape of cybersecurity, the deployment of advanced security measures is crucial for maintaining a robust defense against sophisticated threats. This chapter explores a spectrum of advanced security practices aimed at achieving holistic protection. From the strategic implementation of honeypots and honeynets to essential aspects like asset management, change management, and identity and access management, each facet contributes to a comprehensive security posture.

Honeypots and Honeynets:

Strategic Deception:

Introduction: Unveiling the concept of honeypots and honeynets as strategic deception mechanisms to lure and identify potential attackers.

Deployment Strategies: Analyzing various deployment strategies to optimize the effectiveness of honeypots and honeynets in threat detection and intelligence gathering.

Asset Management:

Inventory and Classification:

Foundations: Emphasizing the importance of maintaining a comprehensive inventory of assets and classifying them based on criticality.

Risk Mitigation: Exploring asset management as a risk mitigation strategy, ensuring that security efforts are aligned with the protection of crucial assets.

Change Management:

Controlled Modifications:

Overview: Understanding change management as a disciplined approach to controlling modifications to the IT environment.

Security Integration: Integrating change management practices with security protocols to minimize the risk of unauthorized changes and vulnerabilities.

Identity and Access Management:

Credential Security:

Identity Protection: Highlighting the significance of robust identity and access management practices in safeguarding credentials and controlling user access.

Multi-Factor Authentication: Examining the implementation of multi-factor authentication as a powerful mechanism for enhancing identity security.

Cloud Access Security Broker:

Cloud Security Oversight:

Role of CASB: Defining the role of Cloud Access Security Broker (CASB) in providing visibility and control over cloud services.

Risk Mitigation: Leveraging CASB to enforce security policies, monitor user activity, and mitigate risks associated with cloud-based applications.

Monitoring and Logging:

Continuous Surveillance:

Importance of Monitoring: Recognizing the critical role of continuous monitoring and logging in the early detection of security incidents.

Incident Response Readiness: Utilizing monitoring and logging data to enhance incident response readiness and facilitate forensic investigations.

Encryption:

Data Confidentiality:

Encryption Fundamentals: Exploring encryption as a fundamental practice for ensuring the confidentiality of sensitive data.

End-to-End Encryption: Implementing end-to-end encryption to protect data in transit and at rest, mitigating the risk of unauthorized access.

Certificate Management:

Key Infrastructure Protection:

Certificates and Keys: Managing digital certificates and cryptographic keys as integral components of a secure key infrastructure.

Renewal and Revocation: Establishing certificate management practices for timely renewal and efficient revocation to prevent security lapses.

Active Defense:

Proactive Security Stance:

Introduction to Active Defense: Shifting from passive to active defense strategies to proactively engage and counter potential threats.

Deception and Countermeasures: Incorporating deceptive techniques and countermeasures to disrupt and neutralize attackers before they can exploit vulnerabilities.

Practice Questions and Answers

Honeypots and Honeynets:

Question: What is the primary purpose of a honeypot in cybersecurity?

a) Active defense against attackers

b) Identifying and luring potential attackers

c) Data encryption for sensitive information

d) Monitoring network traffic for performance optimization

Answer: b) Identifying and luring potential attackers

Explanation: Honeypots are designed to attract and identify potential attackers by mimicking vulnerable systems or services.

Question: How does a honeynet differ from a single honeypot?

a) Honeynets are more complex and expensive

b) Honeynets focus on passive defense

c) Single honeypots are more effective in detecting threats

d) Honeynets consist of multiple interconnected honeypots

Answer: d) Honeynets consist of multiple interconnected honeypots

Explanation: Honeynets are networks of honeypots that work together to provide a broader and more comprehensive view of potential threats.

Asset Management:

Question: Why is asset classification important in cybersecurity?

a) To maximize system performance

b) To identify and prioritize critical assets

c) To introduce vulnerabilities in the network

d) To minimize the complexity of asset management

Answer: b) To identify and prioritize critical assets

Explanation: Asset classification helps in identifying and prioritizing critical assets, ensuring that security efforts are focused on protecting the most valuable resources.

Question: How does asset management contribute to risk mitigation?

a) By introducing vulnerabilities

b) By minimizing system performance

c) By aligning security efforts with critical assets

d) By avoiding inventory updates

Answer: c) By aligning security efforts with critical assets

Explanation: Asset management helps in aligning security efforts with critical assets, reducing the risk associated with the most valuable resources.

Change Management:

Question: What is the primary goal of change management in cybersecurity?

a) To maximize system performance

b) To introduce vulnerabilities intentionally

c) To control and minimize unauthorized modifications

d) To accelerate system vulnerabilities

Answer: c) To control and minimize unauthorized modifications

Explanation: Change management aims to control and minimize unauthorized modifications to the IT environment, reducing the risk of security vulnerabilities.

Question: How does change management integrate with security protocols?

a) By encouraging unauthorized changes

b) By avoiding documentation of modifications

c) By minimizing the complexity of security controls

d) By integrating security checks into the change management process

Answer: d) By integrating security checks into the change management process

Explanation: Change management can integrate security checks to ensure that modifications adhere to security protocols and minimize the risk of vulnerabilities.

Identity and Access Management:

Question: What is the role of identity and access management in cybersecurity?

a) To encourage unauthorized access

b) To introduce vulnerabilities intentionally

c) To safeguard credentials and control user access

d) To avoid user authentication processes

Answer: c) To safeguard credentials and control user access

Explanation: Identity and access management is essential for safeguarding credentials and controlling user access to prevent unauthorized entry.

Question: Why is multi-factor authentication considered a strong security practice?

a) It maximizes system complexity

b) It introduces vulnerabilities intentionally

c) It relies on a single layer of authentication

d) It requires multiple forms of verification for user access

Answer: d) It requires multiple forms of verification for user access

Explanation: Multi-factor authentication requires users to provide multiple forms of verification, adding an extra layer of security beyond a single password.

Cloud Access Security Broker:

Question: What is the role of a Cloud Access Security Broker (CASB) in cloud security?

a) To encourage uncontrolled access to cloud services

b) To monitor user activity in the cloud

c) To introduce vulnerabilities in cloud infrastructure

d) To avoid oversight of cloud services

Answer: b) To monitor user activity in the cloud

Explanation: CASB plays a role in monitoring user activity, enforcing security policies, and providing visibility into cloud services.

Question: How does CASB contribute to risk mitigation in cloud environments?

a) By encouraging uncontrolled access to cloud services

b) By avoiding monitoring of user activity

c) By enforcing security policies and mitigating risks

d) By minimizing the complexity of cloud security controls

Answer: c) By enforcing security policies and mitigating risks

Explanation: CASB contributes to risk mitigation in cloud environments by enforcing security policies and addressing potential risks associated with cloud services.

Monitoring and Logging:

Question: Why is continuous monitoring important in cybersecurity?

a) To maximize system performance

b) To avoid detection of security incidents

c) To identify and respond to security incidents in real-time

d) To encourage unauthorized activities

Answer: c) To identify and respond to security incidents in real-time

Explanation: Continuous monitoring is crucial for identifying and responding to security incidents in real-time, minimizing the impact of potential threats.

Question: How does logging contribute to incident response readiness?

a) By minimizing system performance

b) By avoiding incident detection

c) By providing a record of events for investigations

d) By encouraging unauthorized activities

Answer: c) By providing a record of events for investigations

Explanation: Logging provides a record of events, aiding in investigations and enhancing incident response readiness.

Encryption:

Question: What is the primary purpose of encryption in cybersecurity?

a) To maximize system complexity

b) To introduce vulnerabilities intentionally

c) To ensure the confidentiality of sensitive data

d) To avoid data protection measures

Answer: c) To ensure the confidentiality of sensitive data

Explanation: Encryption is used to ensure the confidentiality of sensitive data by securing it from unauthorized access.

Question: How does end-to-end encryption contribute to data protection?

a) By minimizing system performance

b) By introducing vulnerabilities intentionally

c) By securing data in transit and at rest

d) By avoiding data protection measures

Answer: c) By securing data in transit and at rest

Explanation: End-to-end encryption secures data both in transit and at rest, providing comprehensive protection against unauthorized access.

Certificate Management:

Question: Why is managing digital certificates crucial in a secure key infrastructure?

a) To introduce vulnerabilities intentionally

b) To avoid encryption of sensitive data

c) To protect against unauthorized access and ensure trust

d) To encourage uncontrolled access to digital assets

Answer: c) To protect against unauthorized access and ensure trust

Explanation: Managing digital certificates is crucial to protecting against unauthorized access and ensuring trust in a secure key infrastructure.

Question: What is the significance of timely renewal and efficient revocation in certificate management?

a) To maximize system complexity

b) To introduce vulnerabilities intentionally

c) To avoid encryption of sensitive data

d) To prevent security lapses and maintain trustworthiness

Answer: d) To prevent security lapses and maintain trustworthiness

Explanation: Timely renewal and efficient revocation in certificate management prevent security lapses and maintain the trustworthiness of digital certificates.

Active Defense:

Question: What distinguishes active defense from passive defense strategies?

a) Active defense focuses on avoiding incident detection

b) Active defense encourages unauthorized activities

c) Active defense proactively engages and counters potential threats

d) Active defense minimizes the complexity of security controls

Answer: c) Active defense proactively engages and counters potential threats

Explanation: Active defense involves proactive engagement and countermeasures against potential threats, distinguishing it from passive defense strategies.

Question: How does active defense leverage deceptive techniques?

a) By avoiding deception to minimize complexity

b) By introducing vulnerabilities intentionally

c) By actively engaging and disrupting attackers through deception

d) By relying solely on passive defense mechanisms

Answer: c) By actively engaging and disrupting attackers through deception

Explanation: Active defense leverages deceptive techniques to actively engage and disrupt attackers, minimizing the effectiveness of their strategies.

Conclusion

In the realm of cybersecurity, the pursuit of excellence is an ongoing journey, and the CompTIA Cybersecurity Analyst (CySA+) certification stands as a beacon of proficiency and knowledge. As we conclude our exploration into this certification through the lens of practice questions, answers, and the path to success in the exam, it is essential to reflect on the broader significance of this accreditation.

The journey through the world of CySA+ has been one of rigorous preparation, strategic thinking, and a commitment to mastering the intricacies of cybersecurity analysis. Through a meticulous selection of practice questions and detailed answers, we aimed not only to aid in exam preparation but to foster a deeper understanding of the key domains and principles underpinning the certification.

As individuals pursue the CySA+ certification, they embark on a transformative experience that goes beyond memorizing facts and figures. CySA+ demands a holistic comprehension of threat intelligence, vulnerability management, and the nuanced aspects of securing specialized technologies. The practice questions served as a bridge between theoretical knowledge and practical application, challenging aspirants to think critically and apply their skills to real-world scenarios.

The art of crafting effective practice questions lies in providing not just correct answers, but comprehensive explanations that elucidate the reasoning behind each choice. This approach enables learners to grasp the intricacies of cybersecurity analysis, empowering them not only to pass the exam but to excel in their roles as cybersecurity professionals.

Success in the CySA+ exam is not merely about achieving a passing score; it signifies the attainment of a skill set that positions individuals as adept cybersecurity analysts. It is a validation of one's ability to assess, respond to, and mitigate cybersecurity threats effectively. The practice questions provided a simulated environment for honing these skills, preparing candidates for the dynamic challenges they will encounter in the field.

As the journey concludes, it is crucial for individuals to carry the knowledge gained forward, applying it in real-world scenarios and adapting to the ever-evolving landscape of cybersecurity. The CySA+ certification serves as a testament to one's dedication to continuous learning and professional growth in the face of an ever-changing digital landscape.

In the grand tapestry of cybersecurity, each certified professional adds a thread of expertise and resilience. The pursuit of the CompTIA CySA+ certification is not just a milestone; it is a commitment to fortifying digital landscapes, safeguarding organizations, and contributing to the collective defense against cyber threats.

The journey of a cybersecurity analyst is a perpetual odyssey, and the CompTIA CySA+ certification is a powerful compass guiding professionals toward excellence in this critical field. May your cybersecurity endeavors be ever rewarding, and may you continue to illuminate the path of digital defense.